When
FOOTBALL Was
FOOTBALL

SUNDERLAND

© Haynes Publishing, 2010

The right of Paul Days to be identified as the author of this Work has been asserted
by him in accordance with the Copyright, Designs & Patents Act 1988.

First published in 2010

A catalogue record for this book is available from the British Library

ISBN: 978-1-844259-97-7

Published by Haynes Publishing, Sparkford, Yeovil,
Somerset BA22 7JJ, UK
Tel: 01963 442030 Fax: 01963 440001
Int. tel: +44 1963 442030 Int. fax: +44 1963 440001
E-mail: sales@haynes.co.uk
Website: www.haynes.co.uk

Haynes North America Inc., 861 Lawrence Drive,
Newbury Park, California 91320, USA

All images © Mirrorpix

Creative Director: Kevin Gardner
Designed for Haynes by BrainWave

Printed and bound in the US

When FOOTBALL *Was* FOOTBALL

SUNDERLAND

A Nostalgic Look at a Century of the Club

Paul Days

Contents

Introduction

I was born in Annfield Plain, County Durham in March 1953, grew up as a Sunderland fan and from the age of eight stood on the Roker Park terraces with my father. Aged 12 I was picked by Sunderland to play for one of their junior teams and made my first-team debut for the red and whites when I was just 19 years of age. I therefore have had an association and affection for Sunderland AFC for 50 years!

When I looked through this book it brought back a host of memories for me, not least being picked up every Tuesday and Thursday by a football club bus to take me to training with the juniors at the hallowed Roker Park. We trained round the pitch in those days since a separate training facility wasn't available to us. When the club eventually got a training ground it was at Washington and the Sunderland players helped to build it! Under strict instructions from then manager Alan Brown, a father figure to me, we helped to mix the cement and lay the concrete slabs. The upshot was that players like Cecil Irwin ended up getting burns from the materials used. However, we all mucked in and stuck together as a team, When Football Was Football, doing our best for Sunderland AFC.

It is therefore with great pride that I associate myself with this book and, thinking back particularly to the 1970s, the *Daily Mirror* was the paper that I read to keep me up to date with what was going on in the world of football. In fact most of those I played with or against considered it their tabloid, including lads like Georgie Best who I ended up being good friends with when I left Sunderland.

Micky Horswill

> "I would have died for Alan Brown. Everybody went to the club when they joined Sunderland, but he came to my house and signed me."
>
> Micky Horswill recounts signing for the Black Cats and the debt he owed manager Alan Brown

5

A Canary Saves the Day!
1879-1904

Sunderland and Aston Villa line up for the camera prior to the Black Cats' first home game of the season at Newcastle Road on 9th September 1893. The match was drawn 1-1, the first time the Black Cats had failed to win in 16 home games. The two teams would, as the National Football Museum indicates, provide the world with its first great club rivalry, that would continue well into the 20th century, and an iconic date with destiny in 1913.

1879 Sunderland AFC formed in Hendon by James Allan as Sunderland & District Teachers Association. 1880 The club opened to all professions, not exclusively teachers and the name changed to Sunderland Association Football Club. First recorded game played by the club at home to Ferryhill. 1882 Sunderland AFC move from the Blue House Field to a new ground at Groves Field. 1883 Sunderland AFC move again, this time to the "Clay Dolly Field" at Horatio Street. 1884 Sunderland AFC take up residency at Abbs Field, Fulwell. There they defeat Castletown 23-0 to record the club's highest ever win. Allan scores 12. 1885 Sunderland AFC award their very first testimonial for full-back Watson, who had sustained a compound fracture of the leg in a previous game. 1886 Sunderland move to Newcastle Road, where they would remain for 12 years. 1887 The famous red and white striped shirts are revealed on 24th September 1887 for the match with Darlington St Augustine's. 1888 Allan voted off the Sunderland AFC committee. He forms Sunderland Albion. 1889 Rivalry with Sunderland Albion reaches a nadir when Allan is hit in the eye by a stone after the game and needs hospital treatment. 1890 Sunderland elected to play in the Football League, replacing Stoke City. They lose their first league match 2-3 at home to Burnley. McGregor, Villa director, claimed that "Sunderland had a talented man in every position": Team of all the Talents legend born. 1892 Sunderland crowned Football League champions for the first time following a 6-1 defeat of Blackburn Rovers. Sunderland Albion goes bust. 1893 Sunderland retain their league crown and in doing so become the first team to score 100 goals in a league season. 1894 "Game of 3 halves" against Derby County. 1895 Sunderland AFC win their third league title. Sunderland defeat Fairfield 11-1 in the English Cup. Sunderland become world champions, defeating Heart of Midlothian in Edinburgh. 1896 On 12th August Sunderland AFC become a limited liability company. 1898 Sunderland take up residence at Roker Park. They defeat Liverpool in the first game at the new stadium. 1902 League Championship returns to Wearside for the fourth time. 1903 Sunderland win the Sheriff of London Shield, the forerunner of the Charity Shield. 1904 Sunderland rocked by the McCombie scandal.

Sunderland, founded in October 1879, chose blue for its first stripe in due deference to its original home, the Blue House Field at Hendon, which still exists to this day as a football field. The club's founder, James Allan, sits here in the middle row, second from the left, in 1884. The club nearly went bust in the early years and it was only through the intervention of a committee member who raffled his prize canary that the club was saved!

Red & White Stripes

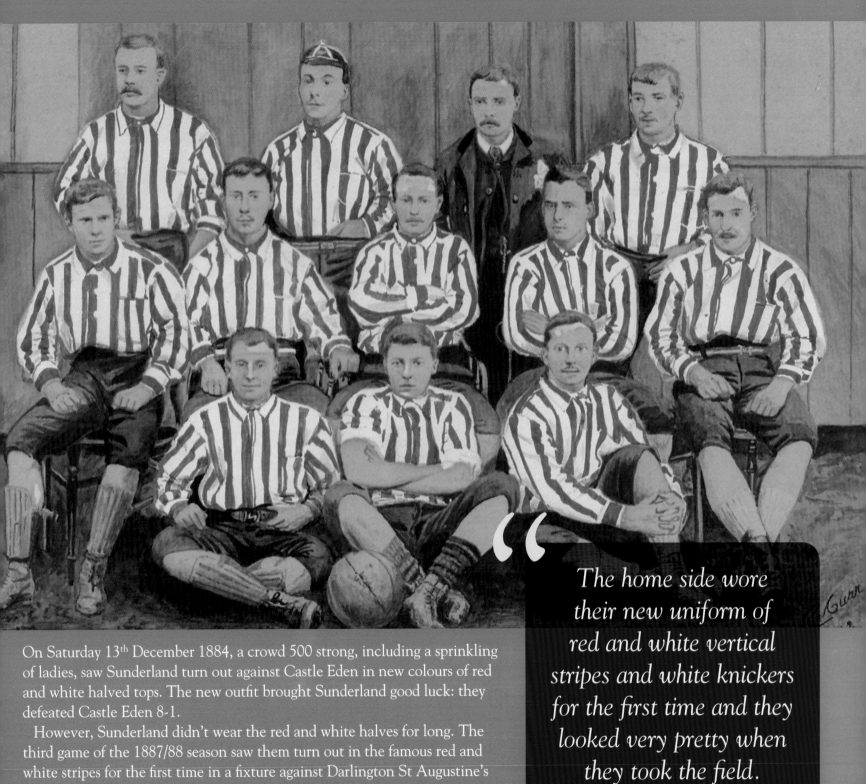

On Saturday 13th December 1884, a crowd 500 strong, including a sprinkling of ladies, saw Sunderland turn out against Castle Eden in new colours of red and white halved tops. The new outfit brought Sunderland good luck: they defeated Castle Eden 8-1.

However, Sunderland didn't wear the red and white halves for long. The third game of the 1887/88 season saw them turn out in the famous red and white stripes for the first time in a fixture against Darlington St Augustine's on Saturday 24th September 1887.

By the middle of 1888 Sunderland AFC's founder James Allan had fallen out with the club and formed Sunderland Albion. The two teams would be bitter rivals until Albion folded because of financial difficulties in August 1892.

> " *The home side wore their new uniform of red and white vertical stripes and white knickers for the first time and they looked very pretty when they took the field.*
>
> Media reports on Sunderland as they took the field in their new strip "

Champions

League Champions

By 1892 not only did Sunderland have a new home, Newcastle Road, but, having been elected into the Football League in 1890, they won the League Championship with a side known as the "Team of all the Talents" in only their second professional season.

Sunderland won their second championship in the 1892/93 season and in doing so became the first team to score 100 goals in a single league season. This was also the inaugural First Division. The 100-goal record would remain until 1919/20 when West Bromwich Albion surpassed the total, although they played 12 more games. Central to the League Championships was manager Tom Watson.

In 1894/95 and for the third time in four seasons, Sunderland would be League Champions, remaining unbeaten at home, scoring 80 goals in 30 league games. Andrew McCombie was a new addition to the first team, joining from Glasgow Rangers. He replaced the original Team of all the Talents captain Johnny Auld at centre-half although he was only 5ft 5in tall.

THE GROUND OF THE SUNDERLAND CLUB.

On 27th April 1895, Sunderland became "world" champions. It was customary at the time for the Scottish League Champions to take on the English League Champions and as both countries were pre-eminent in football at the time the fixtures were billed as a world championship. The Sunderland team left the northeast shortly after 8am and arrived in the Scottish capital, Edinburgh at 12.45pm to take on Heart of Midlothian. Sunderland lunched at the Douglas Hotel, and before the 4 o'clock kick-off took a stroll. The weather was unpromising, but that didn't dampen the enthusiasm of the 10,000 spectators who were treated to an excellent game of football, with the match ending 5-3 in Sunderland's favour.

1901/02 brought Sunderland their fourth championship. The majority of their 19 wins were by a single goal, eight of them 1-0. For that season Sunderland's main rivals were again from Merseyside, this time in the shape of Everton.

Stalwarts of that early side included Scotsmen such as Hugh Wilson.

Early Days of Roker Park

Sunderland players lining up before the opening match in 1898.

ABOVE: Action from an early game against Blackburn Rovers.

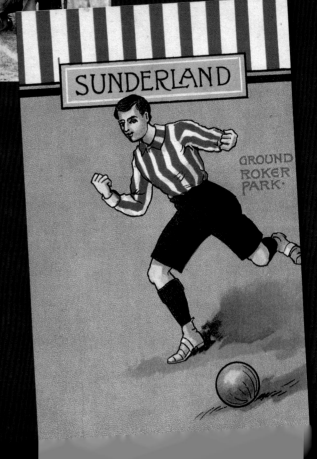

It was the Henderson brothers, one of whom was the Sunderland AFC chairman, who recognized the need for a bigger ground. They negotiated farmland belonging to a Mr Tennant. The agreement was conditional on Sunderland agreeing that houses could be built on part of the land that became Fulwell Road, which meant that, until the houses were built, SAFC had to pay the ground rent on all the land. The Hendersons agreed.

Roker Park was built within a year; the wooden stands within three months. The Clockstand, as it would become known, had 32 steps, no seats and crush barriers for safety. There was a slight drop of about 1 foot from the centre to each side for drainage purposes. The financing of the ground had been made possible with the take-up of 1,700 shares in the club by prominent businessmen in the town.

The President of Sunderland AFC, the Marquis of Londonderry, officially opened the ground on 10th September 1898, turning a gold key in a locked gate that led on to the playing field. Sunderland defeated their first visitors, Liverpool, 1-0. The Roker Park turf was imported from Ireland and was of such quality that it wasn't relaid until 1927, at a cost of £3,000.

–LEGENDS–

Ted Doig

The club had progressed rapidly and was recognized as one of the finest clubs and teams in England. It had boasted some fine players, none more so than goalkeeper Ted Doig.

Sunderland's very first league victory came against West Bromwich Albion on 20th September 1890, at Stoney Lane, a 4-0 triumph that witnessed the debut of John Edward "Ted" Doig in the Sunderland goal. He had been transferred from Arbroath and was known as the "Prince of Goalkeepers". (Incidentally, Doig had been a witness to the Scottish club's 36-0 slaughter of Bon Accord in the first round of the Scottish Cup on 5th September 1885 and had played for them as early as 1883.)

He had a bald head and covered it, always, with a cap held in place by a piece of elastic under his chin! In one famous incident, in a match against Glasgow Celtic, his cap blew off and he is alleged to have raced around the penalty area to retrieve it, rather than the ball! However, he was quite a goalkeeper, and Sunderland were beaten only once at home in six seasons (82 home games) after his arrival.

His transfer was not without controversy, however. While playing for Arbroath he was induced to sign for Blackburn Rovers and played a trial match for them against Notts County. He was subsequently suspended by the SFA and signed for Sunderland once his suspension had expired. This meant he was on the books of two clubs (he was still registered with Blackburn), which resulted in a two-point penalty and a £50 fine for Sunderland AFC.

FOOTBALL –STATS–

Ted Doig

Name: John Edward Doig

Born: 29th October 1866

Died: 7th November 1919

Playing Career: 1883–1909

Clubs: Arbroath, Sunderland, Liverpool

Sunderland Appearances: 456

The Black Cats

In January 1909, Sunderland were going through what was for them a relatively lean spell. It had been seven years since they had won the league, and the team which was to win the Championship with a record number of points and get to the Cup final in 1913 was only just starting to come together.

A 4-1 home defeat to Liverpool on New Year's Day 1909 left the club in the bottom half of the First Division. When the players came into the dressing room the following day before the game against Bury, they found a stray black cat in residence.

Sunderland defeated Bury 3-1, despite Harry Low missing a penalty, and this coincidence started the "lucky black cat" story. A fortnight later when Sunderland went to Bramall Lane and won 3-2 in the FA Cup after being 0-2 down in the second half, the feline mascot was officially adopted by the players and the club's nickname came into being.

> *There has been a big demand for its portrait, more having been disposed of than of all the players put together.*
>
> Media reports of the day indicate the popularity of the football club's new mascot!

Sunderland player Billy Hogg and two unnamed team-mates sitting at a table with a black cat. This is the first known picture of a black cat being associated with Sunderland AFC. Right is a still portrait of the original black cat.

Copyright Photograph by W. A. Culshaw, 119 High St. W., Sunderland.

SUNDERLAND'S MASCOT.

The McCombie Affair

In the close season of 1903/04 Sunderland AFC loaned one of their players, Andrew McCombie, £100 to enable him to start up in business, on the understanding that on receiving a benefit game he would repay the money. Everything came into the public arena in January 1904 when McCombie refused to pay the money back, saying that the £100 had been a gift.

The upshot was that Sunderland AFC were fined £250, six directors were suspended for two and a half years, Alex Watson for 18 months and Alex Mackie three months. McCombie was transfer listed by the club.

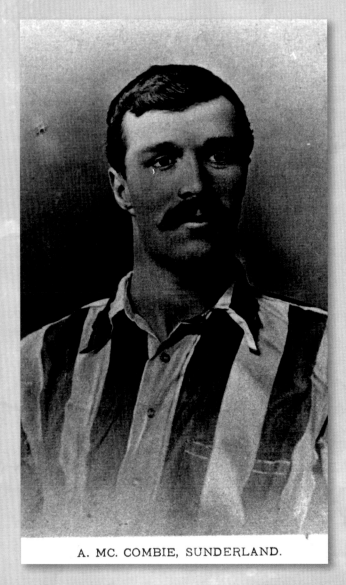

A. MC. COMBIE, SUNDERLAND.

Woolwich Arsenal 0-0 Sunderland, Plumstead, 5th November 1904

The game at Woolwich between the Arsenal and Sunderland was fought out to the end with rare vigour and determination. Both teams had within the space of a fortnight beaten Sheffield Wednesday, the champions, but of the two performances that of the "Reds" was undoubtedly the better achievement, seeing that it was accomplished in the fastness of the Sheffield Club.

Saturday's was a game in which the defence of both sides proved superior to the attack. Anything better than the back play of Jackson and Gray on the Arsenal side, and McCallum and Watson for Sunderland, it would be difficult to imagine. T. S. Rowlandson, Sunderland's amateur goalkeeper, preferred to assist Charterhouse, his old school, in their Charity Cup-tie at Clapton rather than take his position in the Sunderland game. His berth, however, was ably filled by Whitebourne, who rose to a great occasion and gave an admirable display in the Sunderland goal.

During the first half, perhaps, Sunderland had a trifle the best of some very fast exchanges, and yet they were lucky that nothing was scored against them prior to half-time, as Satterthwaite once hit the post with a stinging shot, and Crowe shot through from an off-side position. On the other hand, Sunderland had a couple of goals disallowed for off-side play. Thus, although nothing was scored in the first half, the excitement was maintained at fever heat. In the second half there is no doubt the Arsenal were the better side. They pressed hard, and had bad luck with many good shots. They did not, however, monopolise the attack, and there were at least a couple of incidents in which weak clearances by Ashcroft sadly upset the equanimity of the many thousands of Arsenal partisans.

I should be inclined, perhaps, to attribute the partial success of the Arsenal to the admirable work of the three half-backs, Dick, Sands, and McEachrane, who, although hard pressed during the first quarter of an hour, gradually wore down the impetuosity of the Sunderland forwards, of whom Hogg and Common were the more effective. Satterthwaite and Linward were, perhaps, the best of the Arsenal forwards. Crowe, the youth who made such a sensational début at Sheffield, tried very hard, but still is a trifle short of experience.

Coleman, who played very well indeed, lacked the assistance of Briercliffe, Hunter, his partner, not altogether "nicking in" with the Arsenal inside right. There was a sensational finish to the game, as in the last five minutes four corners accrued to the Arsenal, and each one brought its period of excitement before danger was averted. The game ended with a lucky save by Ashcroft, and thus, after an hour and a half's bustling, strenuous, exciting football, it was "as you were" at the finish.

This was the first time that the two teams had met for league points, and the visit of Sunderland to the capital was eagerly anticipated. It resulted in a record 30,000 attendance in South London.

Just one week later the *Daily Mirror* reporters travelled north to Wearside, taking in Sunderland's fixture with Derby County, a game that Sunderland would win 3-0.

The first *Daily Mirror* match report on Sunderland to carry a picture of the team in action was in the 7th November 1904 edition, which reported on the club's visit to Plumstead, the home of Woolwich Arsenal. The line-up was as follows:

Woolwich Arsenal: Ashcroft, Gray, Jackson, Dick, Sands, McEachrane, Hunter, Coleman, Crowe, Salterthwaite, Linwood.
Sunderland: Whitebourne, McCallum, Watson, Farquhar, Fullarton, Jackson, Hogg, Common, Watkins, Gemmell, Bridgett.

This photograph shows the brilliant Sunderland team who beat Derby County by 3 goals to nil, thus keeping their position at the top of the League list.

Before the match a roving cameraman took this picture of the Sunderland team.

Arthur Bridgett

Arthur Bridgett was one of the pre-eminent strikers of his day. Born in Forsbrook, Staffordshire, in 1882 he was spotted by Sunderland while playing for Stoke, making his debut for the Black Cats against Sheffield United in January 1903. He scored twice in just three minutes against Newcastle in 1908 as his contribution to the 9-1 mauling of the Magpies, and in 348 games for Sunderland scored 166 league and cup goals.

End of an Era

After a quarter of a century, with the departure of Mackie, the McCombie scandal and the arrival of Robert Kyle as club secretary, this was the end of Sunderland AFC's first great era. It had been highly successful, as four League Championships testified, but the one trophy that eluded the club was the FA Cup. This would become their Holy Grail.

Kyle & Co
1905-1928

Sunderland defends a corner at Stoke City on 7th October 1905, with some of the players conscious of the camera! The Black Cats succumbed to a 0-1 defeat. It was a match in which Sunderland ended with just nine men following injuries to both Daykin and Holley. Sunderland players from left to right: Watson, Bridgett, Rhodes, Farquhar, Fullerton and Naisby.

> *The 1920s were great days at Sunderland. And even after I'd left the club I discovered that the fans never forgot you. I couldn't walk anywhere in the town without being stopped by people asking me how I was.*

Billy Ellis recounts what it was like to be a Sunderland player in the 1920s

1905 Bob Kyle becomes manager of Sunderland AFC. 1907 Sunderland draw 5-5 with Liverpool. 1908 Sunderland thrash arch rivals Newcastle United 9-1 at St James' Park. 1909 Newcastle gain revenge by knocking Sunderland out of the FA Cup. Roose becomes the first Sunderland goalkeeper to wear a different coloured top – blue. 1911 Sunderland sign Charlie Buchan. 1912 Sunderland fail to win in the first five league games. 1913 Sunderland becomes League Champions for the fifth time and narrowly miss out on the double, losing the FA Cup final 0-1 to Aston Villa at Crystal Palace. 1914 FA Cup quarter-finalists. 1915 to 1918 No competitive fixtures because of the First World War. 1919 Sunderland win the Durham Senior Cup. 1920 Fifth in the league. 1921 Sunderland thrash Arsenal and Aston Villa 5-1 in consecutive league games. 1922 Warney Cresswell makes his debut. 1923 Sunderland end up runners up in the league. 1924 Third in the league. 1925 Charlie Buchan's last game for Sunderland. 1926 Bobby Gurney makes his debut. 1927 David Halliday top scores with 37 goals for the season. 1928 Johnny Cochrane replaces Kyle in the managerial hot seat, joining from St Mirren.

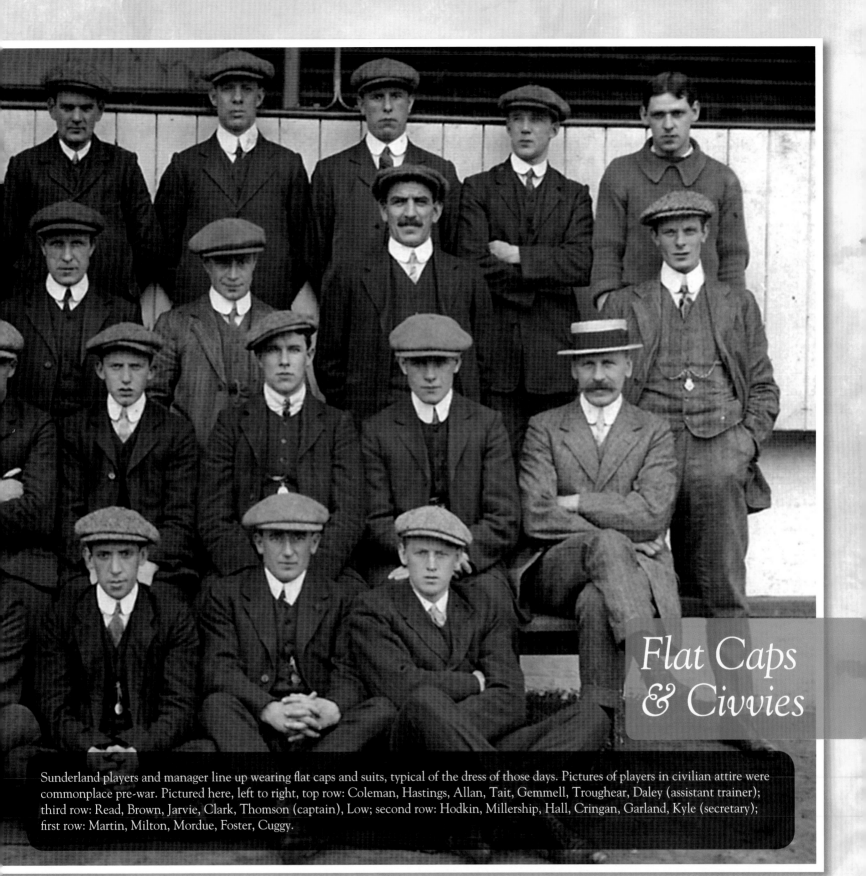

Flat Caps & Civvies

Sunderland players and manager line up wearing flat caps and suits, typical of the dress of those days. Pictures of players in civilian attire were commonplace pre-war. Pictured here, left to right, top row: Coleman, Hastings, Allan, Tait, Gemmell, Troughear, Daley (assistant trainer); third row: Read, Brown, Jarvie, Clark, Thomson (captain), Low; second row: Hodkin, Millership, Hall, Cringan, Garland, Kyle (secretary); first row: Martin, Milton, Mordue, Foster, Cuggy.

Alf Common

Alf Common became the first footballer in the world to be transferred for a four-figure sum when he left Sunderland for Middlesbrough in February 1905. He was born at Millfield in Sunderland and had two spells with the club.

Robert Kyle

The 1903/04 and 1904/05 seasons, for Sunderland, had been dogged by controversy. The McCombie affair, in which Sunderland were judged to have broken wage rules, led to directors and the then manager being banned. As a direct result, in October 1904 new directors took over the club, including "Mr. Sunderland", Fred Taylor, who would serve the club for decades. Secretary manager Alex Mackie left at the end of the 1904/05 season to take up a position with Middlesbrough. On advertising the post Sunderland received 70 applications for the job.

The then caretaker, Fred Dale, was widely tipped to take over, but Robert Kyle had a growing reputation in British football, having won three Irish League titles, two Irish Cups, one City Cup, three County Antrim shields and one Belfast Charity Cup with Distillery. In addition, his Belfast team had defeated Sunderland in a 1903/04 friendly match, which added to his reputation on Wearside. He took up his position at Roker Park in June 1905 and would become the club's longest-serving manager.

Woolwich Arsenal 2-0 Sunderland, Plumstead, London, 21st October 1905

Sunderland travelled on the Friday to Plumstead for their game against Woolwich Arsenal. Included in the team was McKenzie, their new centre-forward from Third Lanark, who supporters hoped would bring a change of fortune. Their hopes were dashed, however, for Sunderland lost the services of the new man early on and with only 10 men they were unable to prevent Woolwich winning the game 2-0.

Woolwich Arsenal: Ashcroft, Gray, Sharp, Dick, Sand, McEachrane, Bellamy, Fitchie, Coleman, Blair, Templeton.
Sunderland: Naisby, Rhodes, Watson, Farquhar, Fullarton, Barrie, Hogg, Holley, McKenzie, Gemmell, Bridgett.

–LEGENDS–

Charlie Buchan

Charlie Buchan was one of the all time Sunderland greats, and pre-war perhaps the finest striker England produced. He stood an impressive 6ft tall and weighed in at 12st 3lbs.

Born at Plumstead in London he started his career with the Northfield club before moving to Leyton Orient, having previously left Arsenal in a row over expenses. Signed by manager Bob Kyle for Sunderland on 21st March 1911 for £1,200, he was just 21 when he played in the 1913 FA Cup final. By the end of his Sunderland career, which lasted some 15 years (four years lost to the war), he was the only Black Cat to have scored 200 league goals. Buchan's career record of 209 league goals for Sunderland has yet to be surpassed.

During the war Buchan served with the Grenadier Guards. On being given lance corporal status he ended up fighting on the Western Front at the Somme, Cambrai and Passchendaele, three of the bloodiest conflicts of that war. That he survived all three to tell the tale is a feat in itself; that he was also decorated for his bravery makes his story complete.

Buchan went on to become both a broadcaster and a journalist with his *Football Monthly* magazine.

FOOTBALL –STATS–

Charlie Buchan

Name: Charles Murray Buchan

Born: Plumstead, London, 22nd September 1891

Died: Beaulieu-sur-Mer, France, 25th June 1960

Playing Career: 1908–1928

Clubs: Woolwich Arsenal, Northfleet, Leyton Orient, Sunderland, Arsenal

Sunderland Appearances: 411

Sunderland Goals: 222

> *I remember thinking particularly of Charlie Buchan, perhaps the greatest of Sunderland football stars, who would have been signing on in the same room.*
>
> Raich Carter reflects on his boyhood Sunderland idol

The Tyne Wear Derby Game, *Early Days*

Sunderland travelled to St James' Park on 1st September 1906 and came away empty handed, losing 2-4.

The 1909 Newcastle United-Sunderland FA Cup third-round tie in progress at St James' Park, which ended 2-2.

Tyne–Wear matches, like most derby games, are not for the faint hearted, and crowd disorder has followed and troubled the fixture since it was first played. Historically, rivalry between the two cities goes back to the time of Cromwell, when each chose a different side to back. Sunderland chose the victorious Roundheads while Newcastle sided with the Royalists.

Newcastle United 1-9 Sunderland, St James' Park, 5th December 1908

Hat-trick heroes on 5th December 1908: Billy Hogg (left) and George Holley (right).
Their place in Sunderland AFC folklore is assured!

The early Tyne–Wear derby games included one at Roker Park. So many people turned up that the crowd spilled onto the pitch, and whilst order was being restored a police horse was stabbed at the Fulwell end. The most famous derby game played between the two sides, however, took place on 5th December 1908 when Sunderland travelled the 10 miles to their bitter rivals and trounced the Magpies 9-1. It remains to this day the highest top-flight victory ever by an away side in the history of English league football.

1913 *FA Cup final, Aston Villa-Sunderland*

Sunderland reached their first FA Cup final after an arduous campaign that saw them defeat Clapton Orient 6-0 at Roker Park in the first round. The game at Manchester City had to be abandoned due to crowd disorder, which was so serious that the *Daily Mirror* saw fit to publish the happenings on the front page together with a montage of pictures. A win in the replayed game was followed by a comfortable victory over Swindon Town.

Sunderland then were drawn to play their arch rivals Newcastle United, and following an epic three-game series of matches the Black Cats made it through to an FA Cup semi-final encounter at Bramall Lane against Burnley. This game also required a replay at St Andrews, which Sunderland won to take them through to the FA Cup final against Aston Villa at Crystal Palace.

SUNDERLAND'S DECISIVE VICTORY.

Clever headwork by Low, of Sunderland, in the Cup-tie against Clapton Orient at Roker Park. The home team won 6—0.

Swindon put up a big effort in the second half to pull their match out of the fire against Sunderland, but they had too much leeway to make up, and were in the end beaten by 4 goals to 2. It was a hard, fast game, decided, however, in the first four minutes, during which Sunderland scored twice.

The first goal was scored by Buchan, after Skiller had made a faulty clearance from Mordue, but Richardson's goal at the end of four minutes was shot with a fast, low ball, out of reach of the Swindon keeper. The third goal, just before the interval, was the result of a bad blunder by Skiller, who ran out to field a long free kick by Gladwin from halfway, the ball bouncing over his head into the net. Richardson scored Sunderland's fourth and last goal two minutes after the breather, from a splendid pass by Martin.

After this it is said Sunderland eased up. At any rate Swindon, who had always been playing well, had more of the game, and first Fleming scored a beautiful goal after beating the backs, and Wheatcroft got through from a scrimmage in front of the Sunderland goal a minute or so later. It was a good game up to the finish, and Lamb, Fleming and Wheatcroft all missed further chances.

Sunderland Playing at Home Fail Beat Newcastle United.

HAY AND WILSON BRILLIA

There were some sensational results in Sat day's four Cup-ties; three visiting teams w and Newcastle United were not defeated at S derland. And perhaps the last was the m surprising result of the lot.

And what a game Sunderland have been looked upon as a wonderful collection of stars, combined into the most skilful club of recent years. So they may be, but they were not able to develop their ultra cleverness in controlling the ball Saturday. Their combination was scattered by the sup play of the Newcastle half backs, and beaten in one st the Sunderland forwards did not put their brains into th work and develop their attack on other lines.

"It was Jimmy Hay's match" was the remark on eve tongue as the great crowd left the ground. The Sund land right wing was never allowed to get going. Buch and Mordue, the paralysing, bewildering pair, were he up as effectually as if they were raw novices, and Jim Hay had the lion's share of the honour.

But that little thickset fellow must not be given the credit. Hugh Wilson, nominally inside left on t Newcastle side, was really assistant left and centre ha and full-back, and I believe he would have been goalkeep too had the rules allowed it, and the necessity arisen. Wilson does not look fast, but his judgment is super and he was always there, either leading the most dangerou of the Newcastle attacks, or putting the tin hat on th attempts of Buchan and Mordue to get into their strid and that upset the Sunderland apple-cart.

So versatile was Wilson in this respect that he an Hay came into violent collision with their heads toward the end of the game, and Hay staggered, got his cleara ing side in, and then went down like a log.

With Buchan and Mordue outgeneralled by this pair o spoilers, Low, the centre half, had a comparatively easy task in dealing with Richardson, and this left the backs and Colin Veitch, the right half, to attend to the Sunder land left wing, and particularly the speedy Martin.

MISTAKEN TACTICS.

Now, Martin has been long enough in fir... he shall not to allow even a b...

TWO GOALS EACH AT NEWCASTLE.

United and Sunderland Again Finish Level in Stirring Cup-Tie.

BRILLIANT HALF BACKS.

NEWCASTLE, March 12.—After two hours' foot ball at St. James's Park this afternoon Newcastle and Sunderland again failed to decide who shall meet Burnley in the semi-final of the English Cup, the scores being two goals each at the finish. There was a huge crowd present, 56,717 people paying £2,547 for admission, and thousands failed to get in the ground. The replay will take place at New castle on Monday next.

As early as seven o'clock in the morning crowds left Sunderland by the workmen's trains and others set out on Shanks's pony to trudge the twelve miles of road which separated the two grounds. Later in the day it seemed that all the conveyances available had been pressed into the service to bring folk from Durham into Northumberland. Bicycles and taxis formed the vanguard of the great exodus, and the town was packed.

It was a great game, and much fine football was given by both sides. Sunderland, on the day's play, were the better balanced side. Their forwards played much better football than they did on the first meeting of the clubs. They swung the ball about more, and in the second half particularly, when they got the measure of the defence, they made some fine movements, though Holley and Buchan were much improved.

Thomson was the hero of the match so far as spectacular effect was concerned. He scarcely put a foot wrong all through, but perhaps the goal honours belong to Sunderland's half-backs. Milton and Gladwin were superb for Sunderland, Gladwin kicking and tackling grandly, and it was just a wee bit unlucky on the team that Newcastle's two goals were led up to by about the only two blunders they made in the match.

McCracken and Hudspeth were also fine for New castle, but McCracken was not allowed to play his put the-man-offside game so much. Cuggy and Low, Sunder land's wing half-backs, bent Thomson fine aid, but the trio they were no better than Veitch, Low and Hay. Lawrence had a lot more to do in goal than Butler. Of the Newcastle forwards Shepherd, who hurt his head, was practically a passenger in the second half. Hibber played finely in the centre, and Wilson was both forward and half-back as on Saturday.

IRRITATING REFEREEING.

The refereeing was irritating, fair shoulder charges bein repeatedly penalised, with the result that at one time good, clean game looked like developing into a scram Had it done so it would have been a pity, for the mate had always a good sporting game. After the fine displa the whole was always governed by Mr. H. Taylor last week the contrast was m marked.

We shall have another mighty match, but I think So derland will win now sooner or later. It is all so go that I do not care how much later. Rutherford and Stewart were unable to turn out that I do not care how much later. The lin confident to a man that they would win. argument was that they played badly in the first ma and were not likely to do so again.

The game started ten minutes before time. Newca pressed at the start, but were not very dangerous, and first incident was a shot by McTavish high over the ba I was told first incident was a shot by McTavish high over the ba succeeded. The players gradually settled down and play became even. From a long centre from Cuggy, Lawrence, and luck The ball hit ing clear, drove the ball against Holley, and luck enough to get went behind, instead of into the goal. Just after It was a nasty kick in the ribs. Fro...

Newcastle now able to field their best side—that when Wilson played on Saturday—and the connections of the club to twenty-fi played on Saturday—and the connections of the club through, and confident to a man that they would win. The lin just these fa argument was that they played badly in the first ma thence it, rel and were not likely to do so again.

it left a mar The game started ten minutes before time. Newca to at least or pressed at the start, but were not very dangerous, and I was told first incident was a shot by McTavish high over the ba

LU...

Newcastle now popular with the Geordies.

BRILLIANT CUP VICTORY FOR SUNDERLAND

Newcastle United Beaten by 3 Goals to Nothing in a Blizzard at St. James's Park—Two Goals for Mordue.

NEWCASTLE, March 17.—After five hours of Cup-fighting Sunderland qualified to meet Burnley at Blackburn in the semi-final round of the English Cup. It was really a wonderful game, and Sunderland should have won by more than 3 goals to 0.

No such an ending could have been expected after the first match at Sunderland, when the Newcastle half backs dominated the play. But from match to match the forwards shook off the attentions of Veitch, Low and Hay, and both when playing with the blizzard at their backs and when facing it they were always too clever for the Newcastle defence. Indeed, Sunderland had many more scoring chances in the second half than they did in the first.

That interest in the strenuous struggle was unabated was evidenced by the fact that as early as nine o'clock crowds of excursionists from Wearside, sporting the Sunderland colours, were parading the streets of the city. It was bitterly cold, and snow showers and sunshine alternated.

An hour before the start a veritable blizzard swept over the district, but by this time there were over 40,000 people on the ground, and, in spite of the rigours of the weather, a steady stream was pouring towards St. James's Park from all quarters of the city.

Sunderland had exactly the same side as played in the two previous games, but Newcastle had to rearrange their team. The backs and half-backs were the same as in the previous matches, but Duncan and Stewart came into the forward line in place of McDonald and Shepherd.

Stewart had played in the first match at Sunderland, so with the exception that Rutherford was absent Newcastle thus played their full strength, which does not lend much colour to the story that they played a reserve side against Blackburn Rovers on Saturday on account of injuries to their players.

Mr. Baker again had charge of the game and refereed badly, tempers being lost on both sides because the players were not allowed to contest the game in a sporting spirit. But Sunderland rose superior to such deplorable conditions, and finer football played under such deplorable conditions.

Holley, at inside left, who would have been playing at Bristol but for this Cup-tie, was the best of a fast, enterprising and virile line of forwards, but now and again the combination of Ouggy, Mordue and Buchan, on the other wing, was cheered to the echo.

Mordue's goal in the second half was the result of this wonderful work, and the Newcastle defenders were left standing still, accomplished and helpless, when the final touch was put on. Richardson was a bustling centre, and Martin was a great winger, doing some fine individual work against McCracken.

Thomson again led his men with rare judgment, and played another stirring game. I should say he is certain of his Scottish cap again. Ouggy and Low were less conspicuous, but sound, and Gladwin and Milton this time made no mistakes. Butler, in goal, had only a couple of anxious times, and on both occasions he got the ball away well. Lawrence made many good saves in the Newcastle goal, and McCracken and Hudspeth both defended splendidly, but McCracken limped a bit in the second half, and was frequently beaten for pace.

The Newcastle halves had an off day. Perhaps they played as well as they were allowed to do, but they were outpaced all the time. The forwards were clever at times, and did better against the wind than with it. Hibbert and Duncan were the pink. McTavish got in some nice work now and again, but these were only a few bouts of brilliant passing such as we expect from Newcastle.

It is still a far cry to the final, but if we get Sunderland and the Villa there, what a game it will be, probably the best on record at the Palace. But you never can tell.

Sunderland won the toss and had the wind in the first half. Newcastle's goal was in danger early on, when McCracken fouled Martin, and three corners fell to Sunderland in the course of the next minute. Play was scrambling at the start, and it was not improved by Mr. Baker at once absolutely putting the veto on fair shoulder charges.

Eight minutes after the start Sunderland scored. The ball was cleverly worked in by Richardson, who passed to Holley. The latter's shot was a soft one, and Low, in trying to kick clear, sent the ball hard against Holley, whence it rebounded through the goal. Just after McCracken brought Buchan down, and both were hurt.

Now and again Newcastle got down against the wind, and danger threatened the Sunderland goal from a well placed corner kick, which Thomson headed away. The Sunderland forwards were now playing fine football, and Martin shot across the Newcastle goal with a good low shot.

Another blizzard swept the ground, and Sunderland, with it behind them, redoubled their efforts. It was now one continuous solo on the whistle, and the players on both sides were rushing it, Wilson and Gladwin having to be forcibly pulled apart by their colleagues.

Wilson, who had kicked Gladwin, got the worst of the encounter and apparently had his ribs hurt in a bear's hug; and so Wilson and also McCracken were both on the injured list before the game was half an hour old.

In a desperate dash on the Sunderland goal Thomson only just cleared. Then Holley got through for Sunderland, but the referee adjudged that he had knocked the ball through, and the point was disallowed.

Against the blizzard the Newcastle defence were superb, but they were hard pushed and did anything to get the ball away. Martin was tripped by Veitch four minutes from the interval, and Mordue scored from the penalty kick, giving Sunderland a two goals lead at half-time.

"Now then, boys, stand on no ceremony; get it away anyhow. There's only three-quarters of an hour to go." So Charlie Thomson as he led his men out of the dressing-room after the breather.

The snow had ceased, and Sunderland started well, Buchan hitting the post from a corner kick. The ball was kept in front of the Newcastle goal, and Buchan miskicked with a goal at his mercy.

Butler once saved the Sunderland goal by throwing the ball behind when three forwards were on top of him, and a couple of corners followed before Ouggy cleared. Newcastle were now making desperate efforts, but the Sunderland backs played with confidence born of a lead of two goals.

Mordue got through once and passed to Richardson right in front of goal, but, although it was a backward pass, Richardson was given offside. Lawrence had to save from Holley, and Butler got the ball away from a close range shot by Hibbert—a lively escape for Sunderland.

More corners fell to Newcastle, but, desperate as was the onslaught of the Newcastle men, the Sunderland defence was just as desperate. After a brilliant run and centre by Martin, both Richardson and Mordue had the easiest of chances of scoring a third goal for Sunderland, but Richardson's shot was a soft one and Lawrence saved at full length. The goalkeeper, however, got a nasty kick in the head from Richardson, who followed up his shot and fell over Lawrence as he lay on the ground.

After some bewildering passing between Mordue, Buchan and Ouggy, Mordue scored a brilliant goal for Sunderland, and settled the issue.

Sunderland had four backs and Newcastle eight forwards in the last few minutes, but it was all over now, and the best team in England had won after one of the most interesting and exciting series of matches in the whole history of the English Cup. It was champion football played by a champion team, which did not, from goalkeeper to outside left, have a single weak spot.

The gate receipts amounted to £2,030, and Newcastle must find some consolation in the face that they have shared £13,000 in this season's competition.

P. J. MOSS.

The Daily Mirror

THE MORNING JOURNAL WITH THE SECOND LARGEST NET SALE.

No. 2,895. Registered at the G.P.O. as a Newspaper. MONDAY, FEBRUARY 3, 1913. One Halfpenny.

ENORMOUS CROWD AT HYDE ROAD, MANCHESTER, INVADES THE FIELD OF PLAY AND STOPS THE CUP-TIE BETWEEN MANCHESTER CITY AND SUNDERLAND.

There were extraordinary scenes at Hyde-road on Saturday, where the Cup-tie between Manchester City and Sunderland had to be abandoned half an hour before owing to the crowd invading the field of play. Sunderland were then leading. It was evident from an early hour that there would be an enormous crowd, and the heap gates were closed half an hour before the kick-off, though thousands were still rolling up. (1) Policemen trying to push back the crowd, who are standing well over the touchline. (2) Mr. Adams, the referee, urging the crowd to keep back. (3) The referee and one of the linesmen trying to clear the touchline of spectators who broke loose on the stand side. (4) Carrying a spectator off the ground on a stretcher. He was injured in the crush. (5) Re-marking the touchline opposite the grand stand. The line had been completely obliterated by the encroaching spectators.

SUNDERLAND WIN THE REPLAYED SEMI-FINAL.

After a great game at Birmingham yesterday Sunderland defeated Burnley by three goals to two. (1) An attack on the Burnley goal. (2) Dawson, the Burnley goalkeeper, saves.—("Daily Mirror" photographs.)

ASTON VILLA

Hardy.

Lyons.   Weston.

Barber.   Harrop.   Leach.

Wallace.   Halse.   Hampton.   Stephenson.

Mr. A.

SOUVENIR
ENGLISH CUP FINAL, 1912-13,
PLAYED AT CRYSTAL PALACE.   LONDON.   APRIL 19th, 1913.

CHARLES THOMSON   JOSEPH BACHE

SUNDERLAND v ASTON VILLA

Printed and published by E. Moran & Sons, Limited, Sunderland.

Martin.   Holley.   Richardson.   Buchan.

Low (H.).   Thomson.   Cuggy.

Ness.   Gladwin.

The English Cup.

Butler.

SUNDERLAND'S TEAM CHOSEN.

Both Sides Training at Home and Both Quietly Confident.

It is hard lines for Sunderland, and particularly so for Milton, that he has not yet sufficiently recovered from his injured ankle to be included in Sunderland's side against the Villa at the Crystal Palace to-morrow

His place will be taken by Ness, the old Barnsley man, who has already visited the Palace in quest of the Cup in the match with Newcastle. Sunderland are lucky to have such a fine player to call upon, seeing that it is the Villa's right wing of Wallace and Halse, the reserve man will have to face.

There was some doubt as to whether Holley would be able to play as he has been suffering from a swollen ankle, but this has greatly improved, and when tested yesterday he was judged sufficiently recovered and got his place. Tinsley will, however, be taken to London ready to take Holley's place at the last moment should it be thought advisable, and Cringan will also accompany the players as reserve.

The players and party will leave Sunderland this morning at 10.25 by a special dining-car, which will make the journey without a stop. The team will put up at Thrale Hall Hotel, Streatham.

Sixteen excursions and special trains will leave Sunderland and the North-East Coast district to-day, carrying, probably, 10,000 enthusiasts.

The Sunderland team have been carefully preparing during the week. They have trained at Roker Park in the usual manner, and are full of confidence in their ability to win the trophy. The directors met yesterday and selected the following team:—

Butler: Gladwin and Ness; Cuggy, Thompson and Low; Mordue, Buchan, Richardson, Holley and Martin.

The selected team is the same as met Burnley twice in the semi-final.

Aston Villa, like Sunderland, have been quietly training at home. They have practised in their own gymnasium, and taken walking and running exercise in the country near Sutton Park. The men are quietly confident of their ability to beat Sunderland. Amongst local footballers they are strong favourites, and the railway companies are preparing for the conveyance of between 15,000 and 20,000 excursionists to London.

The exact composition of the team will not be known until to-morrow morning, but it is hoped that the following full Cup eleven will be available: Hardy; Lyons and Weston; Barber, Harrop and Leach; Wallace, Halse, Hampton, Stephenson and Bache.

Weston is fit again, and Barber and Harrop, who were injured at Bolton on Saturday, have fully recovered.

The team will leave Birmingham to-day and will stay at the Beckenham Hotel, Beckenham. After the match they will go to the Hotel Cecil and stay the week-end.

32

SUNDERLAND

Palace promises to be one of the most interesting and exciting that has been seen for some years, and ... the portraits ... last minute, will face each other on the field. ... Albert Wilkes.]

ASTON VILLA WIN ENGLISH FOOTBALL CUP FOR THE FIFTH TIME.

Sunderland Beaten by a Goal to Nothing at the Crystal Palace.

HARD, STRENUOUS GAME.

Villa Prove the Better Tacticians, and Wearsiders Fail to Find Their Game.

Aston Villa won the English Cup at the Crystal Palace on Saturday by beating Sunderland by a goal to nothing in a game which, although brilliant at times, in nowise came up to the anticipations of those who had looked forward to one of the finest contests ever seen in the last stage of the annual competition. It was the Villa's fifth victory in the competition.

Aston Villa played a hard, bustling game, played it well and won on their merits. Sunderland never found their form, and nervy from the start, developed acute "finalitis," as the stage fright which overcomes teams in their first final is termed. And, as has befallen many another great side at the Palace, they came to grief badly.

Although it was not a match in which the football reached a very high standard of excellence, it was a thrilling picture, set in an extraordinary frame of 121,919 spectators. That we have no ground in the country capable of properly accommodating the vast crowds which flock to see the last act ...

of delight from the Sunderland followers at the failure of this usually certain penalty kick taker.

Players on both sides were frequently offside, and once Hampton got the ball past Butler, amid deafening cheers and counter-cheers followed when it was found that the goal was not allowed. The Villa certainly attacked more than the Sunderland men, but when the latter broke away there always seemed much more danger in their work. But several good chances were missed, once or twice through the weakness of Mordue, who could make but little headway against the rushes of Leach, who bustled into the Sunderland winger what time Weston took the ball and cleared.

This dashing work somehow or other seemed to quite upset the combination between Buchan and Mordue, and the latter had but few real chances, the halves being so taken up with defence that it was only on rare occasions that he got a good pass.

The nearest approach to scoring for some time came from a shot by Low, which Hardy saved cleverly, and, following several free kicks given against Hampton, Mordue forced a corner, from which Hardy made a great save by running out and literally picking the ball from Holley's toes. In the last half-minute of the first half there was another thrilling incident when Hampton, flying between the Sunderland backs, whizzed in a fierce shot, which was only inches wide of the Sunderland goal.

SECOND HALF SHOWER.

The sun had disappeared and a slight April shower was falling when the teams took the field for the second half. Sunderland started really well, and Hardy made another good save from a header by Martin, which seemed certain to find the net. The Villa certainly played a more dangerous game against the wind than with it. Every now and then either Bache or Wallace would outwit the Sunderland wing halves and backs and get in a centre, which the Sunderland defence had great difficulty in dealing with.

Several corners were ...

well, and none could blame them for the defeat. A goal from a corner kick is not much to blame a back for, and the manner in which they covered Butler for the most part shows how well they played.

Butler had not a quarter of the work to do that fell to Hardy, but he made some fine saves. He should, however, have noticed Barber standing unmarked and shouted to one of his comrades to mark him. But perhaps that may be excused him, for how often does a half back score direct from a corner kick?

To a man the Sunderland people, like good sportsmen, admitted that they had been beaten by a better side. At their dinner at the Trocadero in the evening, although disappointment was expressed by several speakers, there was no downhearted or discordant notes struck. The team were congratulated by Mr. McKenna, the president of the League, on their brilliant season; and also by Messrs Walker and Morgan Roberts of the F.A.

Mr. Bentley said he always liked to dine with the losing team to see how they took it, and he said that so cheerful were they that one would almost have thought that Sunderland had won.

Mr. Hamar Greenwood, M.P., in proposing the toast of the club, said that the British race is the only race he knew that did not growl in defeat and chuckle in victory. Mr. Taylor, the chairman, in responding for the club, said that he was disappointed that the Cup was not on the table, but still he hoped the team would win the League, which he considered the blue riband of football, seeing that contest extended over eight months, and the other only eight days or so.

Mr. Taylor went on to say that they had no reason to be downhearted, seeing that instead of having an overdraft of £12,000 at the bank they did not owe a penny. He gave trainer Williams and Mr. Kyle, the manager of the club, and the team his heartiest congratulations on the season.

By the way, a good joke is told of one of Sunderland's leading citizens. Al...

So, Sunderland competed in their first English Cup final and lost, in part due to nerves. This was the closest that they would ever come to winning the double, since they then went on to win the league title, ironically with Aston Villa in close pursuit. At Crystal Palace, and quite inexplicably, the normally steady Sunderland captain Charlie Thomson, folded and in the second half had a running feud with Villa's Hampton. Both were suspended the following season until the end of October. Adams, the referee (who was from Nottingham) was also suspended, having allowed no less than 17 minutes for stoppage time.

Budapest end-of-season Tour

> *During our first game of the tour we had four penalties refused but the referee allowed play to go on. I went to the referee and asked the reason. He replied 'I would not want a great team like Sunderland to score their first goal from a penalty'.*
>
> Sunderland captain Charlie Thomson on the downside of having a good footballing reputation

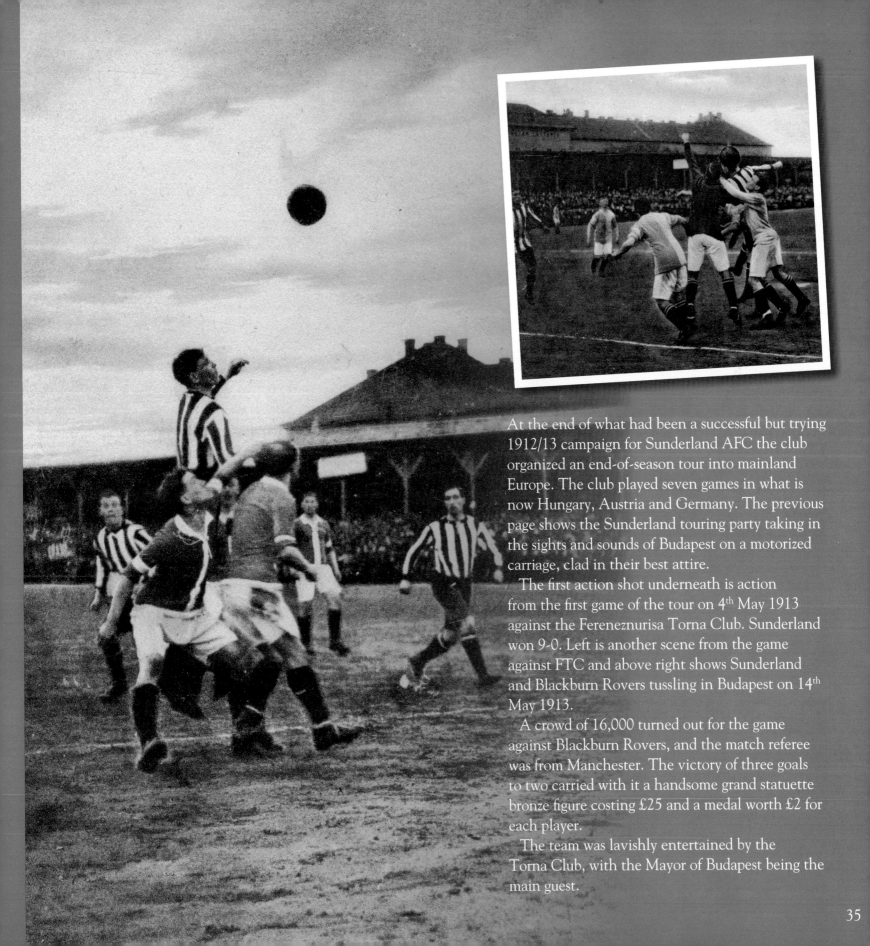

At the end of what had been a successful but trying 1912/13 campaign for Sunderland AFC the club organized an end-of-season tour into mainland Europe. The club played seven games in what is now Hungary, Austria and Germany. The previous page shows the Sunderland touring party taking in the sights and sounds of Budapest on a motorized carriage, clad in their best attire.

The first action shot underneath is action from the first game of the tour on 4th May 1913 against the Fereneznurisa Torna Club. Sunderland won 9-0. Left is another scene from the game against FTC and above right shows Sunderland and Blackburn Rovers tussling in Budapest on 14th May 1913.

A crowd of 16,000 turned out for the game against Blackburn Rovers, and the match referee was from Manchester. The victory of three goals to two carried with it a handsome grand statuette bronze figure costing £25 and a medal worth £2 for each player.

The team was lavishly entertained by the Torna Club, with the Mayor of Budapest being the main guest.

Players Training

Charlie Buchan and goalkeeper George Anderson (standing, left to right respectively) look on as Harry Ness, Frank Cuggy and George Holley get ready to sprint. Note the rudimentary training gear, including thick jumpers!

Military Sports Day, 1918

In both world wars Sunderland gave Roker Park over to the military for physical education training purposes. Here we see the army using the football ground to hold their annual military sports day. The Roker End is in the background.

Sunderland Reserves 1-1 West Stanley Reserves, **30th April 1921**

Sunderland Reserves attack the West Stanley Reserves Fulwell End goalmouth at Roker Park on 30th April 1921. The game ends 1-1 with Vic Shore scoring for Sunderland. Note the Roker End in all its glory – a magnificent sight!

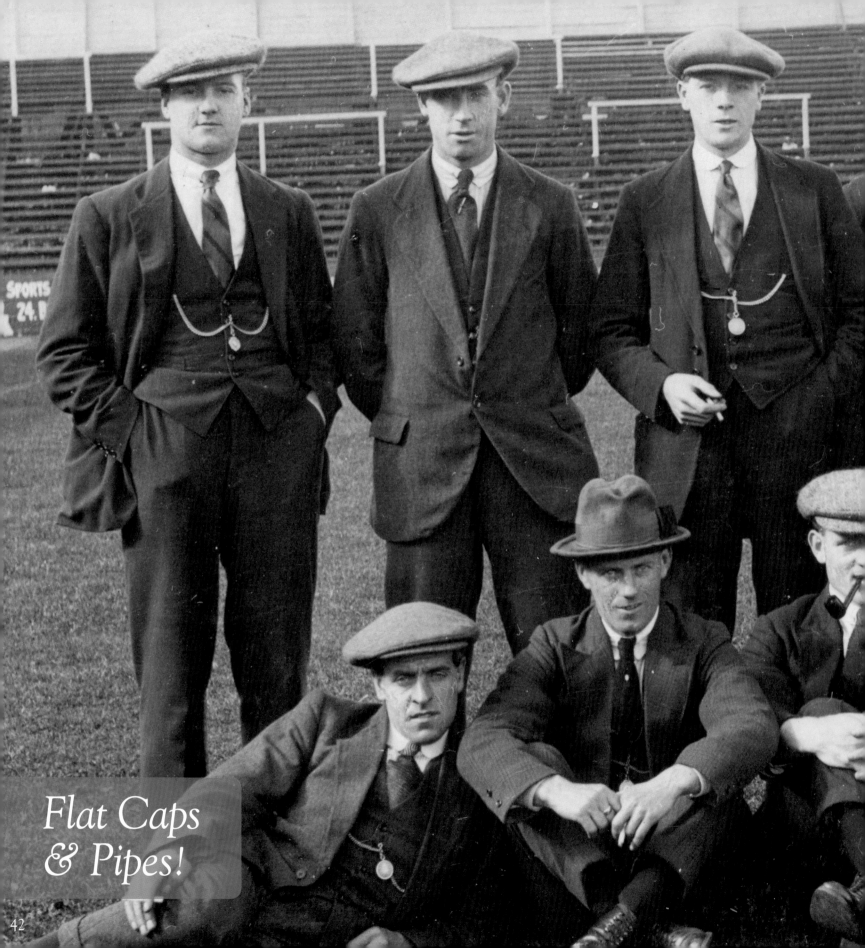

Flat Caps & Pipes!

The Sunderland players line up after training in about 1921/22. Note once again the flat caps, the smart apparel of the day, and the penchant for pipes. The players, left to right, back row: Gregory, Parker, England, Power, Gibson, Stephenson; front row: Stannard, Best, Johnson, Haggan, Hobson.

The Roaring Twenties

Tremelling, Birmingham keeper, dives to the feet of Charlie Buchan, Sunderland inside right, and clears.

Sunderland 2-1 Birmingham City,
24th September 1921

Davis, the Blackburn Rovers' goalie, clears over Paterson's head. Sunderland were the winners by four goals to three.

Blackburn Rovers 0-0 Sunderland,
23rd September 1922

An energetic incident in the hotly contested game between West Ham and Sunderland who won 1—nil.

West Ham United 1-0 Sunderland,
1st September 1923

Sunderland hustling Liverpool's goalie. Liverpool won, 3—1.

Liverpool 3-1 Sunderland, **25th October 1924**

Sunderland 6-1 Sheffield United, **12th September 1925**

Sheffield United's goalkeeper beaten by Halliday (on left), who scored three of the goals which made Sunderland the winners by six goals to one.

West Ham United 3-2 Sunderland, **3rd April 1926**

Just before Sunderland's second goal was scored at Upton Park. Hitting the bar, the ball bounced on the ground.

Buchan, of Arsenal, tries to rob Bell, the Sunderland goalkeeper, in their League match at Highbury. Arsenal won by 2 goals to 1.—(*Daily Mirror* photographs.)

Arsenal 2-1 Sunderland, **17th September 1927**

The 1920s was a scene-setter for Johnny Cochrane's 1930s Sunderland team that would sweep all before it. The hard work during the Roaring Twenties was undertaken by Sunderland manager Robert Kyle, who moulded some fine footballers into an outfit that Sunderland could be proud of.

Sunderland legends such as Charlie Buchan and Joe Kasher, Billy Ellis and Charlie Parker were introduced at Roker Park, with other noted stars being Bobby Gurney and David Halliday.

Local Boys Make Good
1929-1945

The Sunderland squad, directors and manager Johnny Cochrane watch as Raich Carter lifts the FA Cup on the platform of King's Cross railway station in London as the Black Cats make their way home to the northeast with their Holy Grail, the FA Cup.

"*That's a nice wedding present for you.*

The Queen Mother to Raich Carter as he lifted the FA Cup at
Wembley Stadium. Carter was married the week before"

1929 David Halliday is transferred to Arsenal. 1930 Sunderland defeat Liverpool 6-5 at Roker Park. 1931 Sunderland reach the FA Cup semi-final but lose to Birmingham at Elland Road. 1932 Raich Carter makes his debut for Sunderland. 1933 Sunderland attract their biggest ever gate to Roker Park, 75,118 against Derby County. 1936 Sunderland become League Champions for the sixth time. Goalkeeper Jimmy Thorpe tragically dies following the home game against Chelsea. Sunderland defeat Arsenal to take the Charity Shield. 1937 Sunderland win the FA Cup for the first time in the club's history, defeating Preston North End 3-1 at Wembley Stadium. 1942 Sunderland lose the War Cup final to Wolverhampton Wanderers.

Sunderland parade the FA Cup back in the northeast on 4th May 1937.

49

Birmingham City 1-0 Sunderland,
29th February 1929

Sunderland players Adam McLean,
Tom McInally and George Robinson
pose for the photographer before
the 1928/29 league encounter with
Birmingham City at St Andrews.

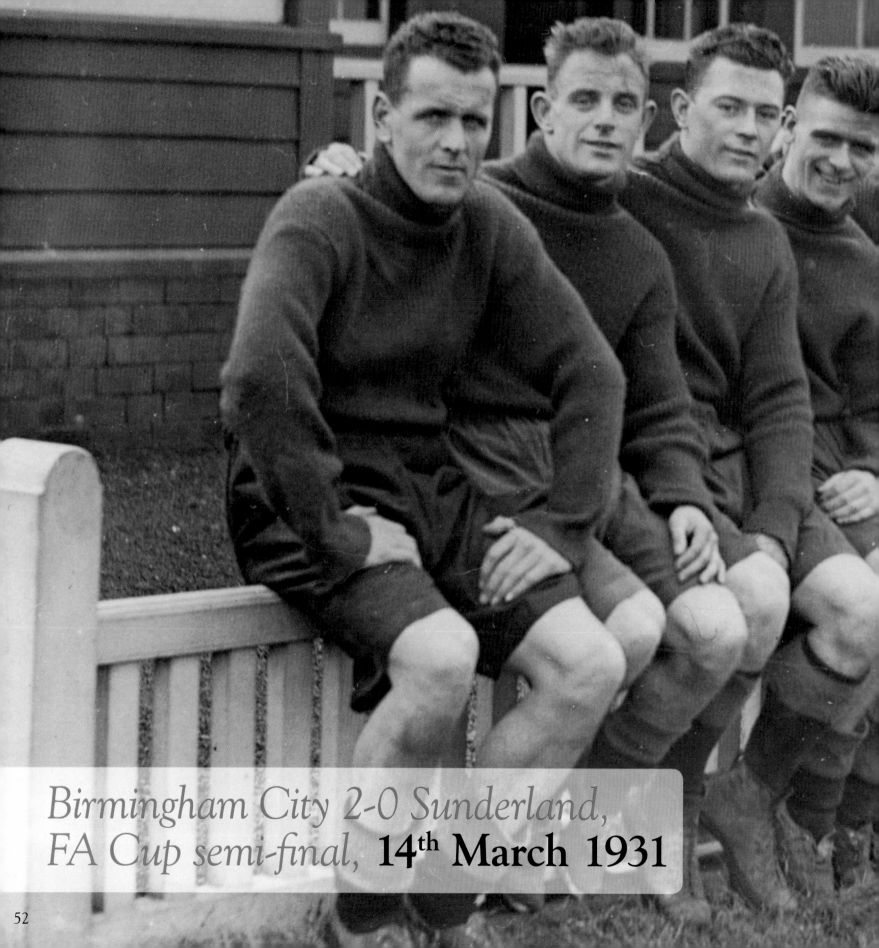

Birmingham City 2-0 Sunderland,
FA Cup semi-final, **14th March 1931**

The Sunderland squad relax at their Southport training camp ahead of the FA Cup semi-final against Birmingham City. Southport was a regular venue for the Sunderland team in the 1930s when they wanted to get away from the football madness on Wearside.

From left to right: MacDougall, Gurney, Shaw, Morris, Connor, Hastings, Leonard, Middleton, Andrews, Murray, Devine, Eden, Reid.

The Glory Years

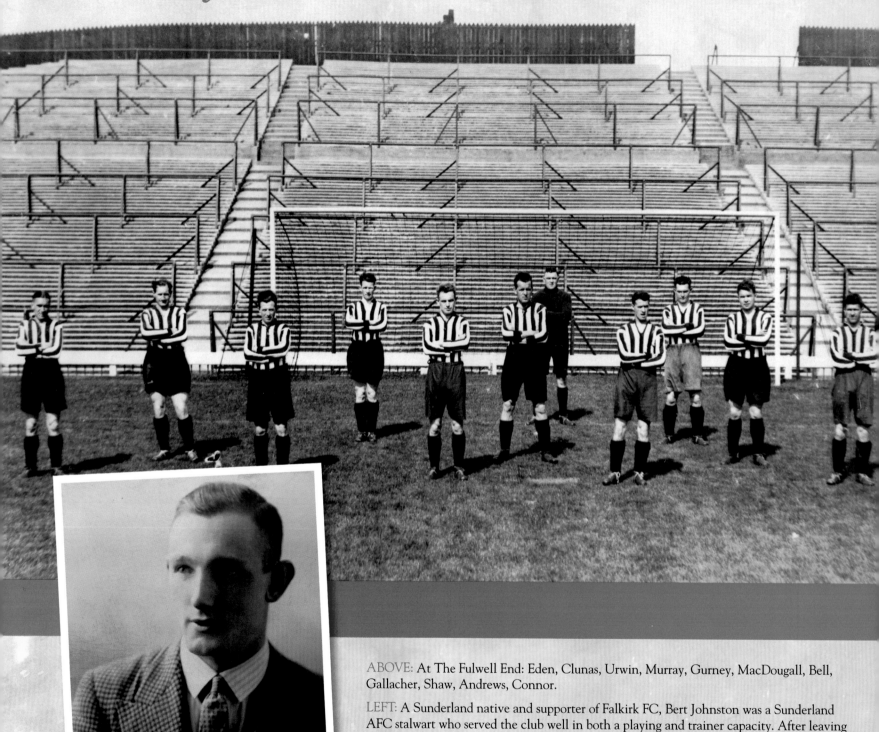

ABOVE: At The Fulwell End: Eden, Clunas, Urwin, Murray, Gurney, MacDougall, Bell, Gallacher, Shaw, Andrews, Connor.

LEFT: A Sunderland native and supporter of Falkirk FC, Bert Johnston was a Sunderland AFC stalwart who served the club well in both a playing and trainer capacity. After leaving school he worked in a bank but left to work in an iron factory that just happened to have a football team. The rest, as they say, is history. Sunderland nearly missed out on his signature from Alva Albion Rovers since another manager waited outside for him as he signed on the dotted line for Johnny Cochrane.

RIGHT: Sunderland players take a stroll, no doubt in preparation for another important game. Trainer Andy Reid takes up a position at the rear in case anyone slacked!

Left to right, front row: Gallagher, Gurney, Davis; second row: Hastings, Murray; third row: Thorpe, Ives; back row: Connor, Thomson, Andy Reid (trainer).

BELOW: Sunderland and the directors line up under the Roker End, probably because of inclement weather. Left to right, back row: Prior, Hall, MacDougall, Clark, Shaw, Middleton, Johnston, Reid; middle row: White, Murray, Hastings, Cochrane, Gurney, Edgar, Taylor; front row: Gallacher, Thomson, Davis, Connor, McNab.

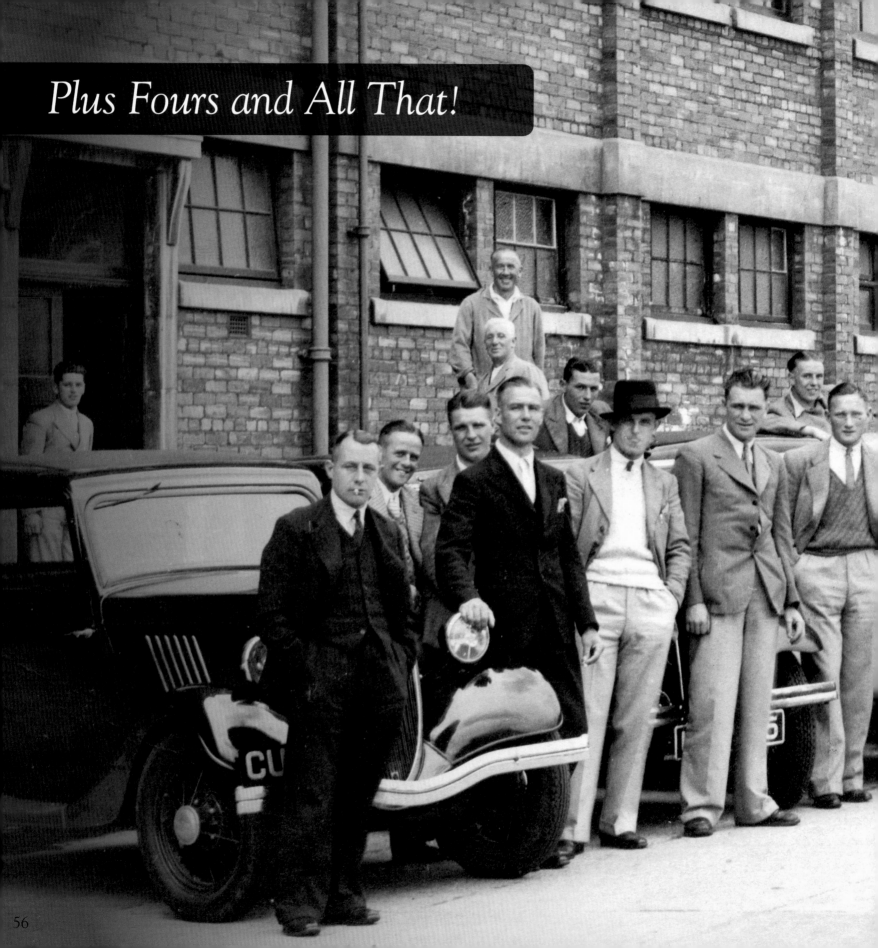

Plus Fours and All That!

Sunderland players line up in August 1936 outside the Roker Park main stand, in their civilian clothes, parading the latest fashion of the day. Note Gallagher with his plus fours!

Left to right, back row: Reid, Dunlop, Middleton, Spuhler, Russell, Royston, Rodgerson, Urwin, Duns, Hastings; front row: Davis, Wylie, Hornby, A Hall, Gurney, Bryce, W Robinson, Gallacher, Thomson, Saunders, Burbanks, Murray, Ainsley, McDowall, Shaw, Clark, Carter, Mapson, Johnston, Cochrane.

FOOTBALL ROUGH PLAY MUST STOP

—Says Inquest Jury

Demand After Player's Death

"The Management Committee of the Football Association should be asked to instruct all referees that they must exercise stricter control over players so as to eliminate such incidents."

THIS was the view of a Sunderland inquest jury last night after they had heard evidence of the Sunderland-Chelsea match at Roker Park on February 1.

They added it as a rider to their verdict at the resumed inquest on James Thorpe, the Sunderland goalkeeper, who collapsed shortly after the match.

The jury found that his death was due to diabetic coma, accelerated by the rough usage he had received

New Style Blamed

When Sir Frederick Wall, formerly secretary of the Football Association, was told of the findings he said:—

"I feel that an inquiry should be held in order to take action upon the recommendations.

"In my opinion, rough play has been developing in recent years. This has been the case more particularly during the past two or three seasons."

"One cause has been the introduction of the new system of re-arranging what one might call the field. I am thinking of the new formation which has been introduced, an attacking centre forward and an attacking half back, commonly called the stopper.

"That, in my opinion, has completely changed the style of play and had been conducive to unfair charging—a dangerous practice."

Coroner on "The Game"

The coroner, in his summing-up, said:—

"You have heard described the game that was played that afternoon. One witness said the game was a disgrace to first-class football. From what I have heard, I quite agree with him. I think it was.

"I feel strongly that some of the men in this game have not been taught as I was taught "When we get First Division football teams playing we expect to get the cream of sportsmanship and the best of play.

"We find players in first-class football who resort to methods that are far from what is to be desired, and they do not really help their clubs or themselves or the game.

"If the referee had been where he should have been, watching the game, the continued ill-treatment to which the goalkeeper was subjected would not have been continued as long as it was—if the referee had done his duty.

"Lost His Grip"

"But he seems, from all accounts, to have lost his grip of the game, and not been able to hold the players in check."

The coroner asked the jury not to pass a vote

(Continued on page 4)

Jimmy Thorpe was a good goalkeeper and his heart and soul were in the game. In our match against Chelsea there was a lot of play in our goalmouth and I heard that Jimmy had been bumped about a bit, although, being up the field I never saw it myself. I remember it most distinctly that when we left the ground Jimmy appeared to be alright and made no complaint of feeling ill, so it was a terrible shock to us when we reported as usual for training on the following Tuesday and learned that he was dead.

Raich Carter comments on the last time he saw his team-mate before his death

Jimmy Thorpe (back row, third from right) lines up with his team-mates for the 26th April 1933 friendly at Roker Park against Racing Club of Paris.

Following the end of Sunderland's match with Chelsea on 1st February 1936, Sunderland's up-and-coming goalkeeper Jimmy Thorpe collapsed at home and spent the following Monday in bed seriously ill as a result of a kick he sustained in the match. He had a head wound, swollen eye and a badly bruised face. He was later admitted to the Monkwearmouth and Southwick Hospital, where he died on Wednesday 5th February.

On Monday 10th February Thorpe was buried at Jarrow Cemetery, the cortège leaving 11 York Avenue, Monkton, the home of his in-laws, at 2.30pm. The funeral was attended by all the Sunderland players and directors, with the former acting as underbearers.

Sunderland were subsequently crowned league champions and on 7th May 1936 the club held a celebratory dinner at which Thorpe's widow and mother were in attendance. Jimmy's championship medal was duly presented to them.

Aged 17, Thorpe had joined Sunderland from his hometown team Jarrow on 26th September 1930. He was talented enough to be selected for the first 11 after just two games for the reserves and was rumoured to be a likely England selection at the time of his death. He made a total of 139 league and cup appearances for Sunderland.

He died aged just 22, leaving a wife May and a three-year-old son, Ronnie.

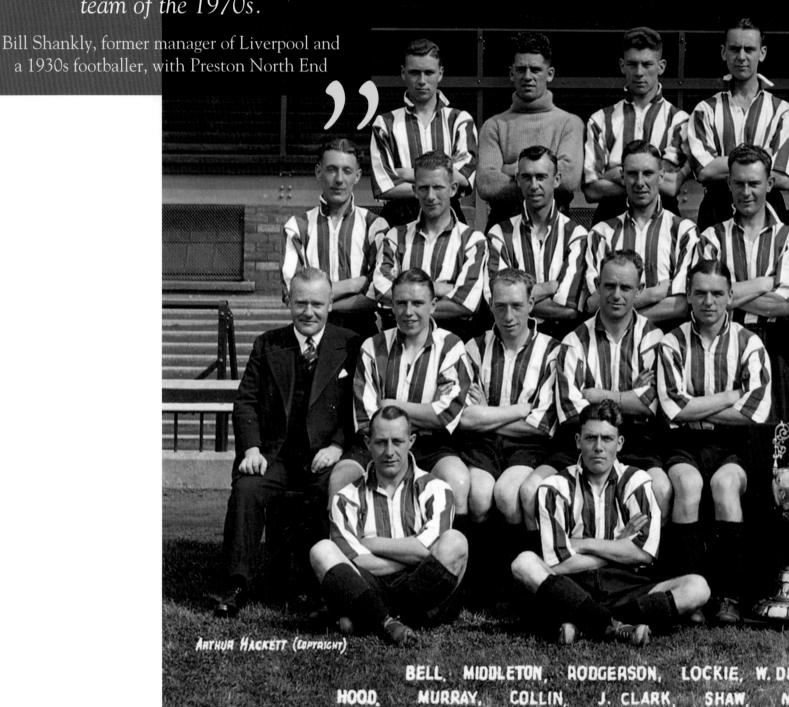

> *In many ways the Sunderland team of 1937 played the same brand of Total Football as the great Holland team of the 1970s.*
>
> Bill Shankly, former manager of Liverpool and a 1930s footballer, with Preston North End

SUNDERLA[ND]
— LEAGUE

ARTHUR HACKETT (COPYRIGHT)

BELL, MIDDLETON, RODGERSON, LOCKIE, W. D[
HOOD, MURRAY, COLLIN, J. CLARK, SHAW,
JOHN COCHRANE (SEC. MANAGER), RUSSELL, McNAB, GURNEY,
DAVIS, THOMSON

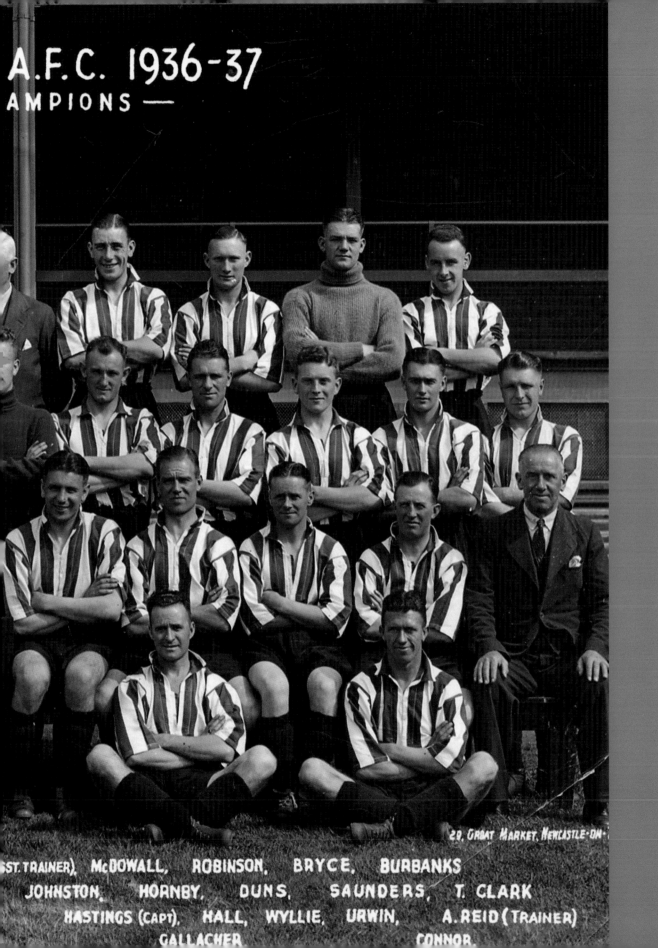

A.F.C. 1936-37
AMPIONS —

29. GREAT MARKET, NEWCASTLE-ON-

ST. TRAINER), McDOWALL, ROBINSON, BRYCE, BURBANKS
JOHNSTON, HORNBY, DUNS, SAUNDERS, T. CLARK
HASTINGS (CAPT), HALL, WYLLIE, URWIN, A. REID (TRAINER)
GALLACHER CONNOR

Sunderland 3-1 Preston North End,
1937 FA Cup final

Sunderland won through to their first FA Cup final after a journey that nearly saw them knocked out by Wolves in the sixth round. Only the intervention of a late goal by Bobby Gurney allowed the Black Cats the opportunity to progress. At Wembley Sunderland started sluggishly and went behind after 38 minutes when Frank O'Donnell scored for the Lillywhites. However, Sunderland were behind for a little more than 10 minutes when first Gurney and then Carter gave the red and whites the lead. Burbanks settled the matter with a third just 12 minutes from time. Sunderland had won the cup for the first time in their illustrious history.

Route to Wembley

January	16th	Southampton	Away	3-2	FA Cup 3
	30th	Luton Town	Away	2-2	FA Cup 4
February	3rd	Luton Town	Home	3-1	FA Cup 4R
	20th	Swansea Town	Home	3-0	FA Cup 5
March	6th	Wolves	Away	1-1	FA Cup 6
	10th	Wolves	Home	2-2	FA Cup 6R
	15th	Wolves	Hillsborough	4-0	FA Cup 6RR
April	10th	Millwall	Leeds Road	2-1	FA Cup S/F

1937 FA Cup final
Preston North End: Burns, Gallimore, Beattie, Shankly, Tremelling, Milne, Dougal, Beresford, O'Donnell (F), Fagan, O'Donnell (H).
Sunderland: Mapson, Gorman, Hall, Thomson, Johnston, McNab, Duns, Carter, Gurney, Gallacher, Burbanks
Referee: Mr Rudd of Middlesex   **Attendance:** 93,495

Raich Carter collects the FA Cup from the Queen.

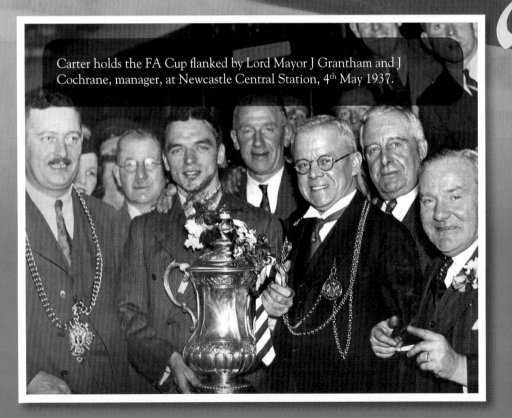
Carter holds the FA Cup flanked by Lord Mayor J Grantham and J Cochrane, manager, at Newcastle Central Station, 4th May 1937.

"

We took things easy and had a quiet time. The peace was solace to the nerves. In the mornings we did a bit of limbering up or played golf, we went for walks in the afternoons and in the evenings we went to the pictures. One day we were taken to Wembley to have a look around so that those who had never been before could familiarise themselves with the ground.

Raich Carter reflects on the days leading up to the final

"

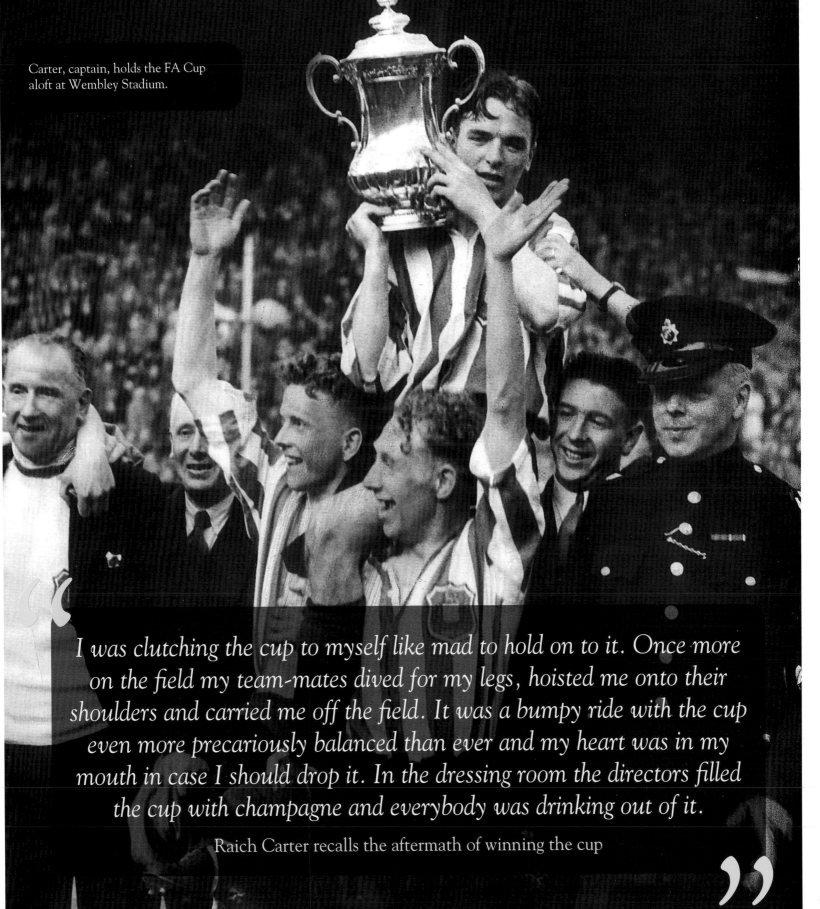

Carter, captain, holds the FA Cup aloft at Wembley Stadium.

" I was clutching the cup to myself like mad to hold on to it. Once more on the field my team-mates dived for my legs, hoisted me onto their shoulders and carried me off the field. It was a bumpy ride with the cup even more precariously balanced than ever and my heart was in my mouth in case I should drop it. In the dressing room the directors filled the cup with champagne and everybody was drinking out of it.

Raich Carter recalls the aftermath of winning the cup "

–LEGENDS–

Bobby Gurney

Bobby Gurney's legendary career at Sunderland started off as another one finished, that of Charlie Buchan. Between them they amassed 450 goals for the club. Gurney played for only one club in his entire career – Sunderland AFC, his hometown club – and along with Bill Murray guided the Black Cats through the period of the Second World War. As loyal servants and football club legends go they don't come any greater than Gurney.

FOOTBALL –STATS–

Bobby Gurney

Name: Robert Gurney

Born: Silksworth, County Durham, 13th October 1907

Died: Sunderland, 14th April 1994

Playing Career: 1925–1946

Clubs: Sunderland

Sunderland Appearances: 390

Sunderland Goals: 228

Bobby Gurney and Raich Carter, both Sunderland legends, carry the FA Cup on to the Roker Park pitch on 4th May 1937.

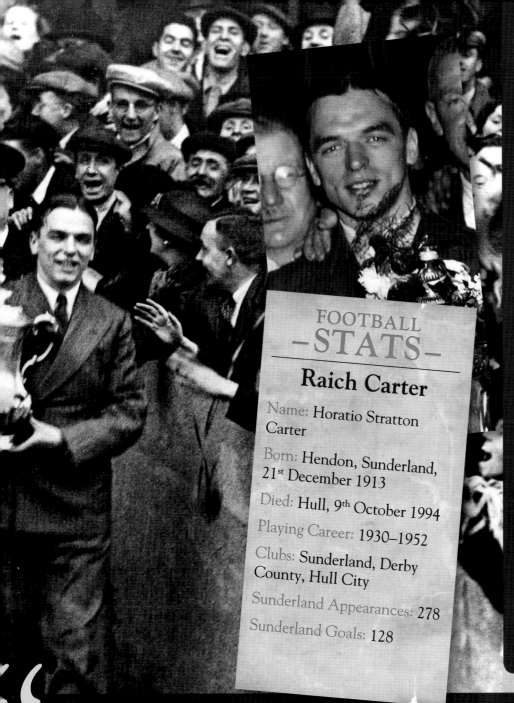

FOOTBALL -STATS-

Raich Carter

Name: Horatio Stratton Carter

Born: Hendon, Sunderland, 21st December 1913

Died: Hull, 9th October 1994

Playing Career: 1930–1952

Clubs: Sunderland, Derby County, Hull City

Sunderland Appearances: 278

Sunderland Goals: 128

-LEGENDS-

Raich Carter

It is fitting that the footballer regarded as perhaps the finest ever to play for Sunderland AFC was born a stone's throw away from where the club was formed, Hendon, a renowned working-class area of the modern city. It was a chance of fate that saw Carter sign for the club after he was inexplicably rejected by Leicester City. That oversight was corrected by Johnny Cochrane, who signed Carter for a £10 signing on fee. Carter went on to become captain and win the Charity Shield, FA Cup and League Championship with Sunderland, the same as his good friend Bobby Gurney. He is still revered by Sunderland fans young and old.

The Second World War would interrupt the world of football from 1939 to 1945. Although there were competitions – indeed Sunderland reached the final of the 1942 War Cup final – the period was littered with a series of guest players turning out for British clubs. Ironically, one of Newcastle United's greatest ever players, Jackie Milburn, guested for Sunderland during this period.

It was a never to be forgotten sight. Sunderland had gone crazy. My arms ached from holding aloft the cup. Every member of the team must have been moved but to me it meant so much more. This was my home town and these were my own folk. I was the local boy who had led the team to victory and had brought home the cup for which they had been waiting for 50 years. What more could any man ask? My happiness could never be more complete.

Carter, Sunderland captain, recalls his emotion on returning to Sunderland with the cup

The Bank Goes Bust
1946-1958

Goalkeeper Harry Threadgold jumps to stop Arthur Wright, Tommy Wright and George Aitken from powering in a header, while Len Shackleton looks on in amusement, with the Clock Stand in the background.

This period in Sunderland AFC's history would be a defining one and perhaps gives a lesson to all football clubs who try to buy the league title. It would herald a big spending era at Sunderland, which became known as the Bank of England Club.

Other clubs would become envious at Sunderland's purchasing power and record of being the only club in England never to have played outside the top flight. However, the club became embroiled in an illegal payments scandal that shook the football world and before the Swinging Sixties started they were relegated.

> "I was Sunderland crazy as a kid.
> They were the only team for me.
>
> Tottenham Hotspur player Ralph Coates reflects on his
> boyhood love of Sunderland AFC"

1945 FA Cup football resumes after the Second World War. 1946 League football resumes. 1948 Sunderland end up just one place from relegation. 1949 Non-league Yeovil Town knocks Sunderland out of the FA Cup. 1950 Third in the league. 1951 FA Cup quarter-final. 1954 Sunderland smash the world transfer record with the purchase of Trevor Ford. 1955 FA Cup semi-final. 1956 FA Cup semi-final. 1957 Sunderland are rocked by an illegal payments scandal that would see players and officials initially banned *sine die* from football in England. 1958 Sunderland relegated to the Second Division for the first time in their history despite winning the final game of the season at Portsmouth.

Arthur Hudgell smacks the ball towards the Roker End goal with the Roker Park main stand on the right and the then uncovered Fulwell End in the background. Hudgell had signed for Sunderland from Crystal Palace in January 1947 for a then record fee for a defender. He would become a stalwart of the club, making 275 appearances in a red and white shirt.

Immediately after the cessation of hostilities the normalization of football began. For Sunderland this meant that pre-war players such as Arthur Wright (left) Len Duns (centre) and Arthur Housam (right) would be joined by other stars to eventually create the "Bank of England Team".

Sunderland AFC has always been a club close to its fans. Here we see an unknown teenage boy and girl meeting Sunderland players Arthur Wright, Jackie Robinson and Fred Hall on the Roker Park pitch in front of the Roker End, in about 1949–50.

Post-war Crowds

Sunderland fans at Roker Park make themselves known at the October 1948 league encounter with Manchester United. Post-war was boom time as far as English football clubs were concerned, and for the Black Cats this was no exception. The 1948/49 crowd average of 45,220 was the highest ever in the history of the football club. It was then surpassed in 1949/50 as over 1 million people passed through the turnstiles.

Chelsea 3-1 Sunderland, Stamford Bridge, 7th September 1949

Medhurst, the Chelsea goalkeeper, has the ball safely in his arms after gathering it from Davis, the Sunderland centre-forward, seen in striped shirt, while Harris, the Chelsea captain, on left is in attendance.

Yeovil Town 2-1 Sunderland, FA Cup fourth round, 29th January 1949

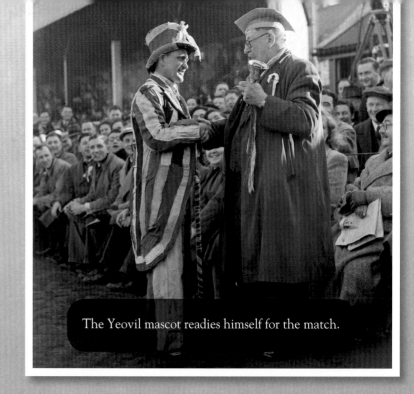

The Yeovil mascot readies himself for the match.

The home fans cheer Yeovil's first goal.

Yeovil's match winner Eric Bryant reflects on his achievement with his young daughter after the game.

In one of the biggest shocks ever in the history of the FA Cup the mighty Sunderland were humbled on the slope of Huish by non-league Yeovil Town. Some 45,000 ticket applications were received for this 16,000-capacity game as the 500-1 outsiders pulled off a minor miracle by holding their First Division opponents to 1-1 after 90 minutes. The unbelievable then became folklore as an extra-time goal from the Glovers player Eric Bryant secured the most famous win in the Somerset club's history.

Following a fine midfield run Dickie Davis, the Sunderland centre-forward, loses the ball to Farm, the Blackpool custodian. Hayward the Seasiders centre-half looks on anxiously.

Sunderland 3-1 Galatasaray,
13ᵗʰ September 1950

Galatasaray's 18-year-old goalkeeper Seren saves magnificently as an onrushing Davis aims to pick up the rebound. A hugely entertaining game saw the Black Cats triumph over their Turkish counterparts at Roker Park. Kirtley had given Sunderland a ninth minute lead and this was added to by Duns, before the Turks pulled a goal back through R Eken on the half-hour. Dickie Davis restored Sunderland's two-goal advantage just before half-time.

Sunderland: Mapson, Hedley, Hudgell, Scotson, Walsh, McLain, Duns, Kirtley, Davis, Shackleton, Reynolds
Galatasaray: R.Seren, Ozkaya, Erdoglu, Seler, B.Eken, Tokac, Ozis, Tucaltam, R.Eken, Tilin, Varrol
Referee: Mr R Wood of Sunderland
Attendance: 14,830

Sunderland 1-0 Red Star Belgrade, Festival of Britain, Roker Park,
16th May 1951

Sunderland captain Willie Watson shakes hands with his Yugoslavian counterpart before the Festival of Britain game at Roker Park.

The Belgrade goalkeeper Lovic collects the ball safely as Dickie Davis moves in on goal.

To celebrate recovery from the Second World War the Festival of Britain took place in May 1951, with a number of uplifting events. Included was a series of football matches. Sunderland AFC's contribution to the festivities was a friendly against crack Yugoslav side Red Star Belgrade at Roker Park, a game that the hosts would win 1-0 with a goal from Ivor Broadis after 34 minutes. Here we see the Red Star President Mita Miljkovi signing an agreement of friendship with the Lord Mayor (Sir) Jack Cohen in attendance as well as Sunderland manager Bill Murray and the club chairman Stanley Ritson. The Red Star representatives include the manager, Ljubiša Broćić.

Dickie Davis

Sunderland centre-forward Dickie Davis meets a cross at the Fulwell End as part of pre-season training in 1950. Davis had been signed from a Midlands no league club shortly before the Second World War broke out and went on to feature over 150 times for Sunderland. His 25 league goals during the 1949/50 season saw him end the campaign as England's top First Division goalscorer.

Arsenal 3-0 Sunderland, 1st September 1951

Sunderland finished outside the top nine in only 13 of their first 50 league seasons – a remarkable record. Consequently, games such as this one against Arsenal in September 1951 drew huge crowds as Sunderland, the only team never to have played outside the top flight, brought to town a galaxy of stars such as Trevor Ford, Billy Bingham, Ivor Broadis and Len Shackleton. However, on this occasion Bob Robinson the goalkeeping understudy to Johnny Mapson could do little to stem the Gunners attacks as Sunderland lost 0-3 in front of a mammoth crowd of 66,167. Sunderland, of course, had set a Highbury ground record when 73,295 turned up to see the visit of the Black Cats in March 1935.

Training

George Aitken, Tommy Wright, Arthur Wright and Len Shackleton in pre-season training, August 1952, with the Roker End in the background.

Aston Villa 3-0 Sunderland, 1st September 1952

Sunderland's Jackie Stelling watches as Johnny Dixon of Aston Villa heads the ball goalwards. The 1952/53 season saw the end of Sunderland's indifferent home form; they lost only once all season at Roker Park, unfortunately against northeast rivals Newcastle United. Of significance was the debut of Stan Anderson, 4th October 1952, at home to Portsmouth.

‑LEGENDS‑

Len Shackleton

Known as the Clown Prince of Soccer, Shack was an artist with the ball.

Favouring an inside-left position he gained only five England caps, in the main due to a perceived anti-establishment stance. This was reinforced in his autobiography when he left a blank page for the chapter entitled "What the average director knows about football".

Len was on Arsenal's books as an amateur, but began his professional career with his hometown club Bradford after the war. In 1946 he made a £13,000 move to Newcastle United, scoring six goals on his debut. In February 1948 Sunderland acquired his services from the Tyneside Club after parting with a world-record fee of £20,050.

"Joining Sunderland was the best thing I ever did," recalls Shack, who in time formed part of the "Bank of England Club".

The clown prince of soccer attracted massive crowds wherever he played. An ankle injury in 1957 eventually brought a turbulent and eventful career to a close.

Len Shackleton shoots past Everton's Corbett during the 1948 league encounter at Roker Park.

Newcastle people always tell me that I'm biased towards Sunderland but really I've nothing against Newcastle; I don't care who beats them!

Shack reveals his first love

FOOTBALL
–STATS–
Len Shackleton

Name: Leonard Francis Shackleton

Born: Bradford, 3rd May 1922

Died: 27th November 2000

Playing Career: 1940–1957

Clubs: Bradford, Newcastle United, Sunderland

Sunderland Appearances: 348

Sunderland Goals: 101

Floodlights!

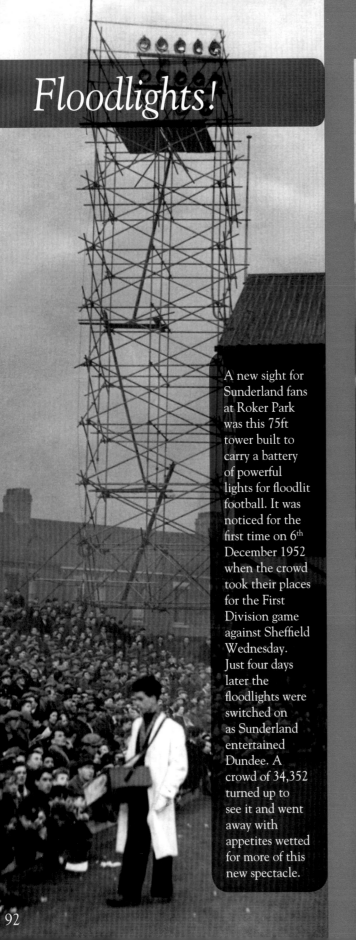

A new sight for Sunderland fans at Roker Park was this 75ft tower built to carry a battery of powerful lights for floodlit football. It was noticed for the first time on 6th December 1952 when the crowd took their places for the First Division game against Sheffield Wednesday. Just four days later the floodlights were switched on as Sunderland entertained Dundee. A crowd of 34,352 turned up to see it and went away with appetites wetted for more of this new spectacle.

Fulham 0-1 Sunderland, Craven Cottage,
12 April 1952

A 57th-minute goal by Len Shackleton in West London gave Sunderland both points. From a 7-1 hammering of Huddersfield Town at Roker Park the day before, this made successive victories for the Black Cats against the bottom two clubs in the First Division.

Fulham: Black, Dodgin, Lowe (R), Macaulay, Taylor, Lowe (E), Hinshelwood, Robson, Stevens, Brennan, Mitten.
Sunderland: Mapson, Marston, Hedley, Watson, Hall, Aitken, Bingham, Davis, Ford, Shackleton, Wright (T).

Bank of England

Fred Hall signed from Blackburn Rovers in August 1946. Hall was an impressive centre-half who clocked up over 200 appearances in a red and white shirt. He eventually became captain of the side and featured as a reserve in the victory international for England against France.

Jack Jones: having guested for many clubs during the Second World War, including Sunderland, Jones was officially signed from Everton in December 1945. He played just one season for the Black Cats before taking his place, for many years, on the Roker Park coaching staff.

Stan Lloyd: signed from Durham Schools during the Second World War, Lloyd's career was handicapped because of the hostilities; he moved on to Grimsby in August 1948, having made 24 league appearances for the club.

Sunderland 1-0 Swansea Town, FA Cup fifth-round replay, Roker Park, 23rd February 1955

Sunderland advanced to the sixth round after a replay against Swansea Town. It was Charlie "Cannonball" Fleming who scored the only goal of the game shortly after half-time.

Sunderland: Fraser, Hedley, McDonald, Anderson, Daniel, Aitken, Bingham, Shackleton, Fleming, Chisholm, Elliott
Swansea Town: Evans, Willis, Thomas, Charles, Kiley, Burgess, Allchurch (L), Griffiths, Medwin, Allchurch (I), Jones

The inquest starts in the Burnley defence as Ken Chisholm, Sunderland's No. 11, turns away delirious having watched his team-mate Billy Elliott score the winning goal that took the red and whites through to a fourth-round encounter with Preston North End. The goal was scored with just five minutes of the tie remaining. The winner, a header, was made by Stan Anderson. It was doubly sweet for Elliott, playing against his old team-mates from Turf Moor. The win was made possible, however, by Sunderland's Welsh international Ray Daniel, who had the game of his life for the home side.

The RJ Schaefer Trophy

The RJ Schaefer Trophy gets a polish from Dorothy Watson in the Roker Park boardroom, 10th June 1955. It was won as a result of Sunderland's 1-1 draw with FC Nuremburg on the end-of-season tour of North America, the game played at Ebbets Field, New York on 17th May 1955, the home of the Brooklyn Dodgers Baseball team.

Sunderland goalkeeper Fraser hits the mud as Manchester City's winning goal was scored by Clarke after 57 minutes as Anderson, among others, looks on. Despite the muddy pitch both sides put on a tremendous display.

Manchester City: Trautmann, Meadows, Little, Barnes, Ewing, Paul, Fagan, Hayes, Revie, Johnstone, Clarke.
Sunderland: Fraser, Hedley, McDonald, Anderson, Daniel, Aitken, Bingham, Fleming, Purdon, Shackleton, Elliott.

> *I thought we were worth a draw. Our players put up a great fight and certainly had more of the play.*
>
> Sunderland chairman, Ted Ditchburn

–LEGENDS–

Charlie Hurley

On 26th September 1957 Charlie Hurley strode into Roker Park to begin a career that would span 12 seasons and 401 appearances. When originally asked by Millwall whether he would like a move, he initially turned Sunderland down. The £18,000 transfer was sealed thanks to the apparent persuasiveness of Sunderland manager Alan Brown, who had been alerted to his potential by the former Millwall manager, Charlie Hewitt.

His Sunderland career met with a disastrous start; a 7-0 rout by Blackpool, coupled with his scoring an own goal on his debut, was quickly followed by a 6-0 thrashing from Burnley. Charlie had been unfortunate enough to have competed against centre-forwards who would later go on to represent England. In Ray Charnley and Ray Pointer, Blackpool and Burnley had strikers of the highest quality. It was a baptism of fire for Hewitt.

Away from Sunderland, Charlie made his debut for Eire at the age of 20, having been unable to make an international call-up due to injury one year earlier. Overall he would gain 40 caps for his native country, 33 while on Wearside, and would have the honour of captaining them.

While the 1963/64 season was special for Sunderland AFC, resulting in promotion, it was also personally highly satisfactory for "King Charlie" as he became known on Wearside. Only the great Bobby Moore prevented Hurley from becoming Football Writers' Player of the Year; the runners up placing truly testifying that at his peak there was no finer centre-half in English football.

RIGHT INSET: Leading from the front; Hurley followed by Cecil Irwin

Hurley comes back out on to the pitch having achieved the 1964 promotion.

Charlie Hurley out-jumps the Everton defence and heads across the goalmouth.

BELOW INSET: Devoted family man, Charlie with his wife Joan in 1963.

> " *I can remember driving up to Sunderland in my first car, a Ford Consul, and wondering just how far I had to go. I thought I was driving to the end of the world.* "
>
> Charlie Hurley, having signed for Sunderland, reflects on his drive up to the northeast

FOOTBALL
–STATS–

Charlie Hurley

Name: Charles Joseph Hurley

Born: Cork, Eire, 4th October 1936

Playing Career: 1953–1972

Clubs: Millwall, Sunderland, Bolton Wanderers

Sunderland Appearances: 401

Sunderland Goals: 26

Cause for celebration!

Young Sunderland fans celebrate outside St James' Park as they witness the Black Cats sixth-round FA Cup victory at the home of their bitterest rivals, Newcastle United. Bill Holden scored both goals in front of a mammoth crowd of 61,474. The win took Sunderland into an FA Cup semi-final at Hillsborough, where things didn't work out quite so well for the Black Cats: the Blues triumphed 3-0.

Alan Brown

When Alan Brown took over at Sunderland in 1957 he had been a good player with the Lancashire club Burnley, having featured for them in the 1947 FA Cup final, as captain, against Charlton Athletic. When he took over he became the football club's first English manager for over 60 years, since Tom Watson. He was only the eighth Sunderland manager in the club's long history.

> *Soccer is the biggest thing that's happened in creation, bigger than any 'ism' you can name.*
>
> Alan Brown, on the People's Game

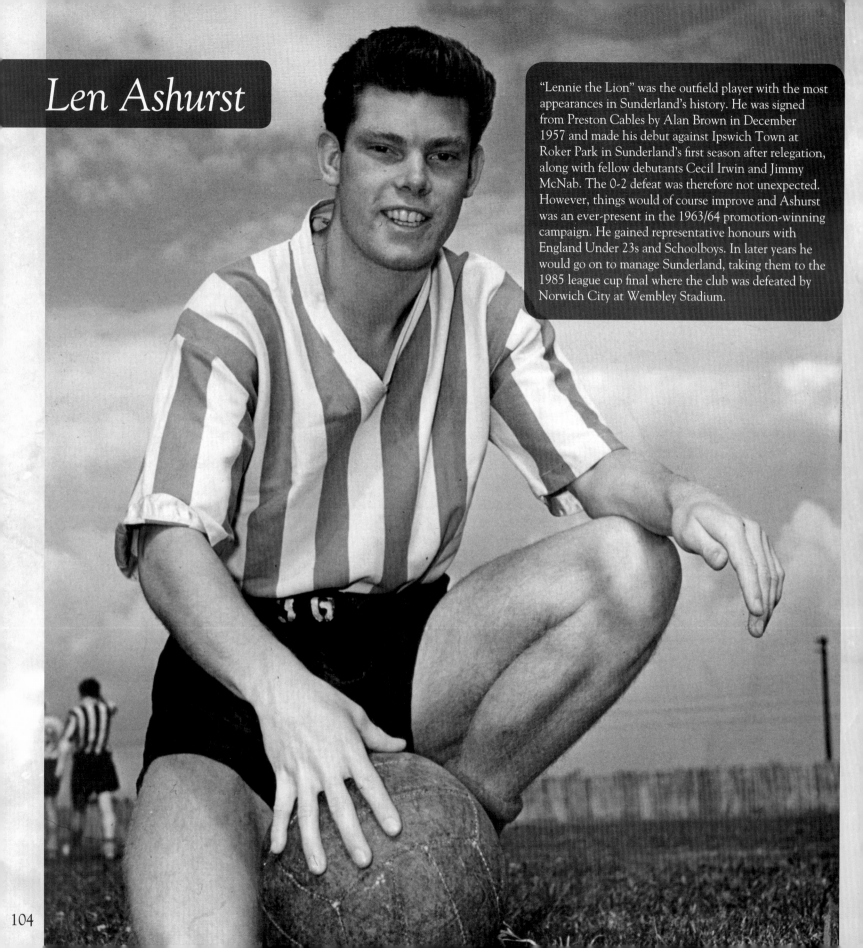

Len Ashurst

"Lennie the Lion" was the outfield player with the most appearances in Sunderland's history. He was signed from Preston Cables by Alan Brown in December 1957 and made his debut against Ipswich Town at Roker Park in Sunderland's first season after relegation, along with fellow debutants Cecil Irwin and Jimmy McNab. The 0-2 defeat was therefore not unexpected. However, things would of course improve and Ashurst was an ever-present in the 1963/64 promotion-winning campaign. He gained representative honours with England Under 23s and Schoolboys. In later years he would go on to manage Sunderland, taking them to the 1985 league cup final where the club was defeated by Norwich City at Wembley Stadium.

Illegal Payments Scandal and First Relegation

Stanley Ritson (left) was a member of the Sunderland Board of Directors who was caught up in the club's illegal payments scandal. News of the scandal broke in 1957: it involved irregular payments over the purchase and return of bails of straw to cover the pitch, with residual monies being used to break the maximum wage structure. As part of the initial inquiry Ritson was among the people forced to resign. However, when it was judged that the Football League had acted ultra vires Ritson was re-instated and resumed his place on the Board of a club he loved so much. Yet the scandal had a devastating effect on the club, since just one year after the debacle started the club were relegated for the very first time in their history. Their proud record of being the only English league club never to have played outside the top flight was over, despite a last day win at Portsmouth. Ironically, it was Leicester City, managed by former Sunderland star David Halliday, who stayed up at Sunderland's expense.

It was truly the end of an era at Sunderland AFC, and time for the club to rebuild.

Wembley Wonderland
1959-1973

When **FOOTBALL** *Was* **FOOTBALL**

"

We enjoyed every minute of the cup run. If there were any trick or magic to it, it was just that we lapped it up and always made sure that the pressure was on sides such as City, Arsenal and Leeds. We didn't feel any pressure. The players were laughing all the time. Later after the final someone referred to us as the team who laughed their way to the FA Cup.

Bob Stokoe gives a tip for good management

"

1973 – The Leeds United players look dejected as Sunderland celebrate Ian Porterfield's 31st-minute goal in the 1973 FA Cup final. In the background the famous Roker Roar go wild!

1959 Sunderland's first season outside the top flight starts badly as they lose their first game 1-3 to Lincoln City. 1960 Sunderland play their first game in the league cup at Brentford. 1961 Sunderland lose in the sixth round of the FA Cup despite an epic game against Spurs at Roker Park. 1962 Sunderland miss out on promotion following a last-day draw against Swansea Town. 1963 Sunderland reach the league cup semi-final where they are knocked out by Aston Villa over two legs. 1964 Sunderland promoted from the Second Division. 1966 Sunderland host World Cup matches at Roker Park. 1967 Sunderland is franchised and play as the Vancouver Royal Canadians in a close season North American league. 1968 Sunderland win at Old Trafford on the last day of the season and deprive Manchester United of the First Division title. 1969 Charlie Hurley plays his last game for Sunderland. 1970 Sunderland suffer relegation once again. 1971 Colin Todd is transferred to Derby County for a record fee between two British clubs. 1973 Sunderland win the FA Cup against all the odds, defeating Leeds United 1-0 at Wembley Stadium. Ian Porterfield scores the only goal of the game.

The squad that won the cup:

Guthrie, Halom, Watson, Montgomery, Pitt, Malone, Young, Hughes, Tueart, Kerr, Horswill, Porterfield.

Ernie Taylor

Sunderland-born Ernie Taylor played for four league clubs: Newcastle United, Blackpool, Manchester United and his hometown club Sunderland. He played for three clubs in three FA Cup finals, winning with Newcastle in 1951 and as inside-forward partner to Stanley Matthews for Blackpool in 1953. In 1958 he was given special dispensation to join Manchester United after the Munich disaster, and got a runners-up medal in the final against Bolton. The ex-submariner had played in an early round for Blackpool. A little Napoleon of an inside-forward, he was a gifted pass master, but was unfortunate to win his one and only England cap in the 6-3 thrashing by the Puskás -propelled Magical Magyars of Hungary at Wembley in 1953.

Sunderland 2-1 Arsenal, Roker Park, FA Cup third round, **7th January 1961**

Arsenal centre-half Mel Charles and Sunderland centre-forward Lawther in a mid-air clash as they strive for possession of the ball.

Liverpool goalkeeper Slater looks surprised as the ball lands in the back of the net from a Hooper shot which put Sunderland one up.

Sunderland 1-1 Tottenham Hotspur, 4th March 1961

Sunderland fans queue up outside Roker Park for tickets for the FA Cup sixth-round game against Tottenham Hotspur.

ABOVE: Sunderland players Fogarty, Lawther, Anderson and Hurley jump for joy when Willie McPheat scores the opening goal to put the Black Cats ahead.

LEFT: Sunderland fans invade the pitch following McPheat's goal as the Spurs players, heads down, look dejected. The crowd of 61,336 were convinced that the Black Cats were on their way to a semi-final appearance, but Dillon scored for the visitors with little more than 10 minutes remaining.

Spurs would win the replay and go on to win the double.

–LEGENDS–

Stan Anderson

Signed in June 1949, Stan Anderson would go on to become one of the players with the most appearances in a Sunderland shirt, outfield-wise matched only by Len Ashurst. A schoolboy international, he turned professional with Sunderland in 1951 and soon became an accomplished right-half, going on to gain full representative honours for England. He gained the distinction of not only playing for the three northeast clubs but also captaining them. His transfer to Newcastle United caused a sensation and was only possible due to the fine form shown by Anderson's understudy, Martin Harvey.

FOOTBALL –STATS–

Stan Anderson

Name: Stanley Anderson

Born: Horden, County Durham, 27th February 1934

Playing Career: 1949–1966

Clubs: Sunderland, Newcastle United, Middlesbrough

Sunderland Appearances: 447

Sunderland Goals: 35

FA Cup 1961, sixth round, Sunderland 1-Tottenham 1 at Roker Park. The ball's off the picture but the expressions tell the hopes and fears of the men who watch it. There's a look of hope and a look of hopelessness. Is it a goal, or isn't it? Bobby Smith of Spurs caused the moment of worry, but the shot flashed wide. The Sunderland players from left to right are: Hurley, Ashurst, Wakeham (goalkeeper), Jimmy McNab and Stan Anderson (extreme right).

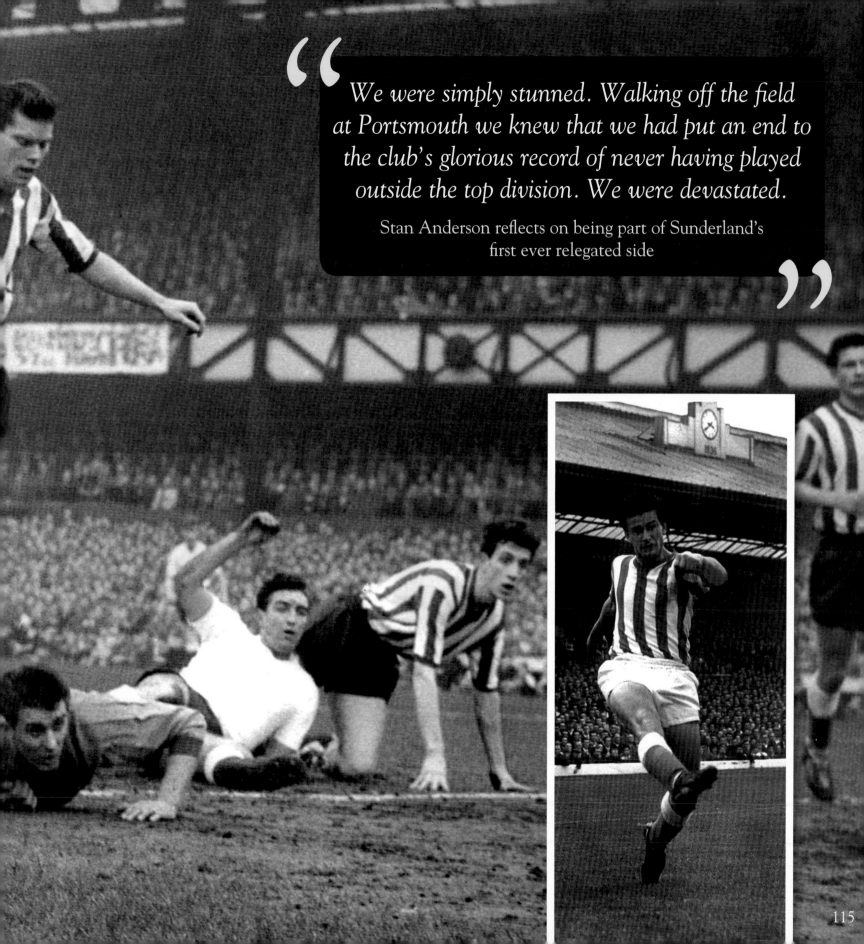

> "We were simply stunned. Walking off the field at Portsmouth we knew that we had put an end to the club's glorious record of never having played outside the top division. We were devastated.
>
> Stan Anderson reflects on being part of Sunderland's first ever relegated side"

Norwich City 3-1 Sunderland, 16th September 1961

Sunderland's Colin Nelson battles with Norwich City's Bill Punton in the Second Division encounter at Carrow Road.

The 1961/62 campaign commenced with two new signings in the form of Brian Clough and George Herd. The club would be almost invincible at home, gaining 37 out of a maximum 42 points at Roker Park. However, failure to win at the Vetch Field on the last day of the season saw the red and whites miss out on promotion.

Jimmy McNab

Jimmy McNab and his bride Miss Sylvia Keeley, of Abingdon Street, Sunderland, after their wedding at St Benet's Roman Catholic Church, Monkwearmouth in May 1962. McNab was a hugely popular figure on Wearside, making over 300 league and cup appearances for Sunderland, mainly at left-half. Born in Scotland he signed from Kilsyth Rangers in August 1956. He would eventually transfer to Preston North End, with whom he won a Third Division championship medal in the early 1970s.

McNab proudly shows off his son Neil after the baby's christening in May 1963.

Leeds United 1-0 Sunderland, Elland Road, 25th August 1962

Jimmy McNab, Charlie Hurley and Cecil Irwin battle for the ball with Leeds United legend John Charles. Over McNab's shoulder is a youthful Billy Bremner, who scored the winner in a match watched by 17,753. Leeds United had yet to become a force in Europe, and the ground looks very different from today.

Sunderland took the field for their final match of the 1962/63 season knowing that a draw against Chelsea, who lay third would be enough too see them promoted. Sunderland lost at Roker Park in front of nearly 50,000 and were pipped to the two promotion places by the Londoners, on goal difference, and Stoke City. It was all too much for one Sunderland fan, who buries his head in his hands, reflecting no doubt on what might have been.

The Men Who Shaped Sunderland AFC

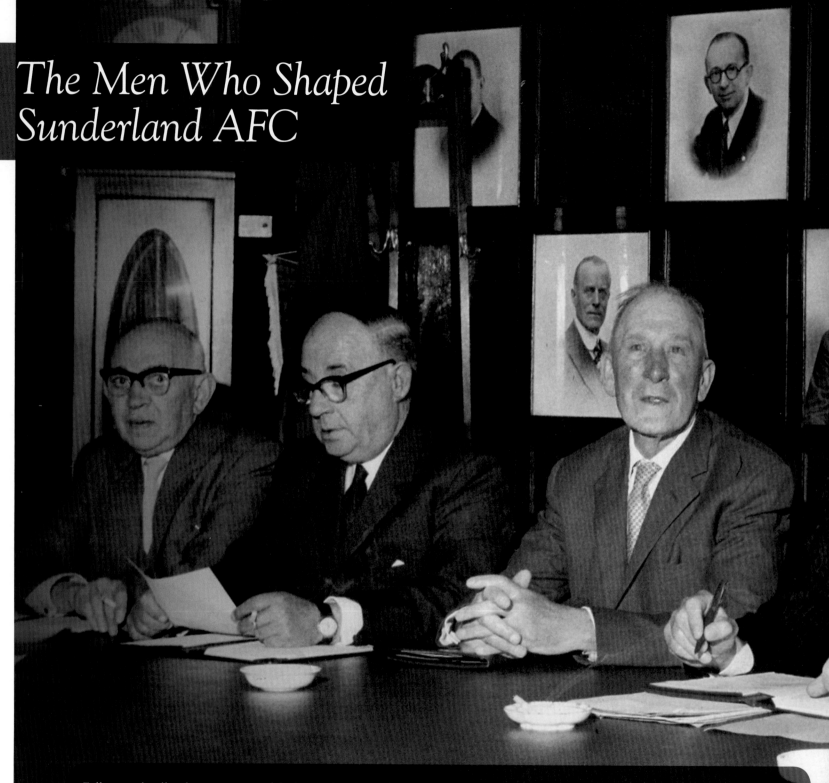

Following the illegal payments scandal of 1957 that dragged on for what seemed like an eternity, it was a nucleus of local businessmen who guided Sunderland through a difficult transitional period for the football club. On 8th July 1963, before the Board and shareholders meeting that day, the following directors were pictured in the old Roker Park boardroom: left to right, Jack Cooke, Jack Parker, Stanley Ritson, Syd Collings, L W Evans and John Turnbull. Note the pictures of the previous chairmen, stretching right back to the turn of the century inlaid in the oak panels behind the directors.

121

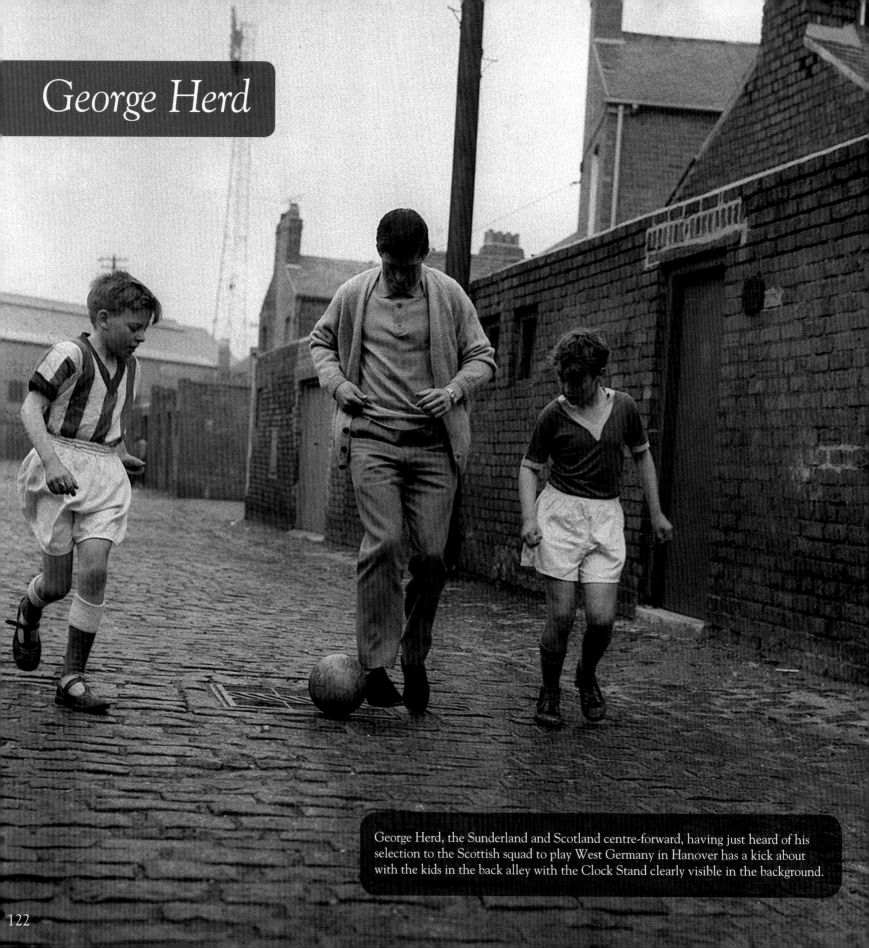

George Herd

George Herd, the Sunderland and Scotland centre-forward, having just heard of his selection to the Scottish squad to play West Germany in Hanover has a kick about with the kids in the back alley with the Clock Stand clearly visible in the background.

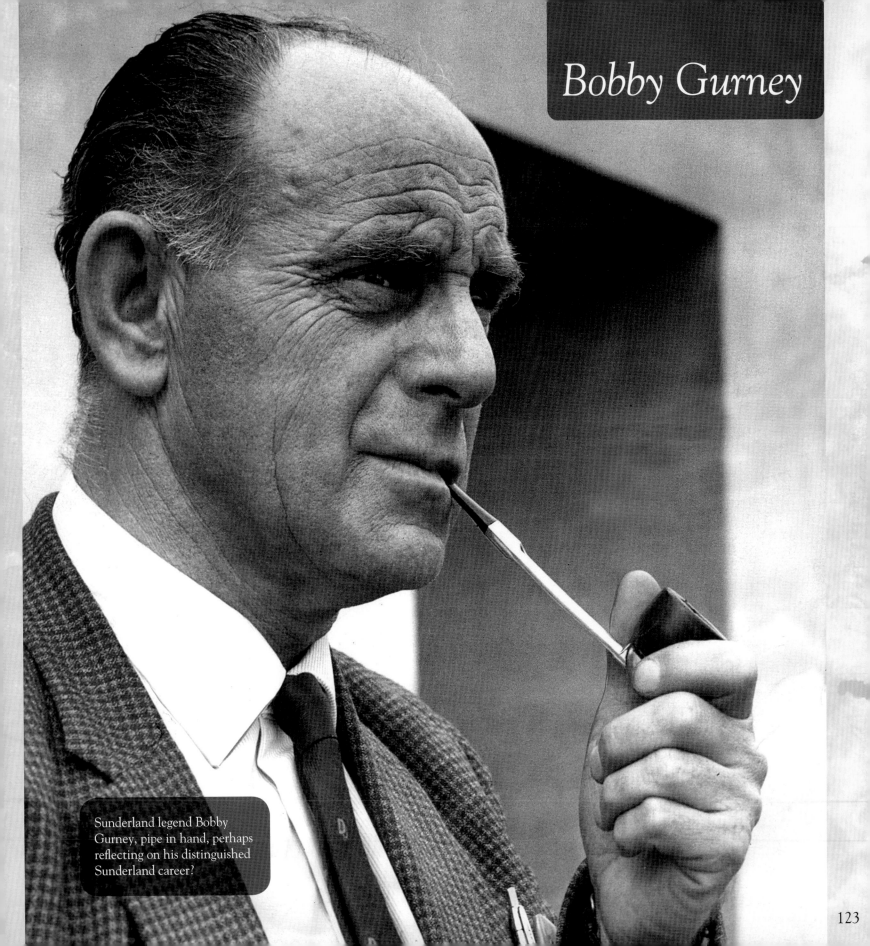

Bobby Gurney

Sunderland legend Bobby Gurney, pipe in hand, perhaps reflecting on his distinguished Sunderland career?

A First Promotion!

The Sunderland players celebrate on the Roker Park pitch after achieving promotion following a 2-1 win over Charlton Athletic on 18th April 1964. From left to right, the players taking the plaudits of the crowd are: Sharkey, Crossan, Mulhall (behind Crossan) Irwin, Hurley (on McNab's shoulders), McNab, Montgomery, Harvey, Ashurst, Usher and Herd.

–LEGENDS–

Brian Clough

Brian Clough needs little introduction to English football fans. His persona was legendary and his goalscoring exploits even more so. Supremely confident in his own abilities, Clough scored an incredible 274 goals in just 251 games for Middlesbrough and Sunderland before a cruciate knee injury sustained against Bury on Boxing Day 1962 effectively finished his career. Although he made a return to first-team action at Roker Park, he called it a day and took up a career in management with Hartlepool United, having at first been on Sunderland's training staff.

Clough in typical pose as he scores for Sunderland against Leeds United at Roker Park on 9th September 1961. He scored both goals that day in a 2-0 Sunderland win, and in his first season on Wearside he notched five hat-tricks!

FOOTBALL –STATS–

Brian Clough

Name: Brian Howard Clough

Born: Middlesbrough, 21st March 1935

Died: Derby, 20th September 2004

Playing Career: 1952–1964

Clubs: Middlesbrough, Sunderland

Sunderland Appearances: 74

Sunderland Goals: 63

> *The best goalscorer in England had been sold for £42,000.*
>
> Brian Clough comments on his transfer from Teesside to Wearside in July 1961

Clough turns up outside Roker Park on crutches in March 1963 and receives encouragement from waiting supporters and a local policeman!

Brian Clough steps back out onto the Roker Park pitch in a pre-season friendly against Huddersfield Town on 15th August 1964, his first game back for Sunderland since his Boxing Day cruciate injury in the match against Bury in 1962.

"
We did have a lot of good players at Roker Park but I don't think there was one of us who was on the same wavelength as Jim. The problem we had was that he was too clever for the rest of us. He was always two moves ahead of the other lads who were playing alongside him. He was an exceptional player one of those guys you come across only once in a lifetime. I never did play with anyone better than he was.

Billy Hughes on the genius that was slim Jim Baxter
"

Jim Baxter was signed for Glasgow Rangers in May 1965 for £72,500, and at the time was widely regarded as one of the best players in Britain. Unfortunately, the Sunderland fans only saw sporadic outbursts of his undoubted talents. This picture shows Baxter in action against his great nemesis, Glasgow Celtic, in an August 1965 pre-season friendly at Roker Park. The game became famous not just for the 0-5 thrashing handed out to Sunderland but for the fact that some of the Scots fans didn't return home for days after the match finished!

Sunderland 2-1 Sparta Rotterdam, Roker Park, 14th August 1965

Nick Sharkey puts Sunderland 1-0 up against Sparta to give the Black Cats a 1-0 half-time lead in a game watched by 20,226. Kemper scored for the Dutch side in the second period, but Baxter made the win safe, despite missing a penalty (see page 131).

1966 World Cup

At FIFA's 1963 world conference in Rome, England was chosen ahead of both Spain and Germany to host the 1966 World Cup; 1963 was the centenary of the FA, so it was appropriate that the country that gave the modern game to the planet should be chosen. The four groups of four played at various venues with Group 4 playing at Ayresome Park and Roker Park. The latter was also chosen as a venue for a quarter-final match.

At Roker Park temporary seating was put in place for the now roofed Fulwell End and permanent seating for the Clock Stand. The pitch was also extended. Furthermore, the ticket office, club administration and a hospitality suite were built to accommodate not only the increased number of dignitaries during the competition, but to enable Sunderland AFC to expand once the tournament was over. Flagpoles at the back of the Roker End housed the colours of the competing nations, including of course the FIFA insignia.

USSR-Italy, 16th July 1966. The Soviet team waves to the fans following the playing of the national anthems.

USSR-Chile 20th July 1966; an overenthusiastic Chilean photographer is removed from the pitch by a policeman as Chile score.

Sunderland 1-1 Manchester United,
9th November 1968

Sunderland's Martin Harvey hits the mud trying to stop Manchester United star George Best from getting a shot in on goal during their league match at Roker Park.

Montgomery saves brilliantly from George Best as Cecil Irwin, Martin Harvey and Charlie Hurley look on.

The Fulwell End

Roker Park covered in straw, 23rd January 1964.

The framework all ready for the new stand being erected at the Fulwell End of Roker Park, 29th July 1964.

The Fulwell End, "the Kop" for Sunderland fans, where by the 1960s the majority of the crowd-chanting would emanate. Many fans would start off supporting Sunderland in the Roker End and gravitate to the Fulwell as they grew into adolescents.

BELOW: A snow covered Roker Park, 15th January 1966.

BEWARE OF THE GROUNDSMAN

Sunderland 1-1 Newcastle United, Roker Park,
31st August 1968

An eagerly anticipated early season game against Newcastle United witnessed a bumper 49,428 to turn up for the First Division clash at Roker Park. However, a crush at the Fulwell End saw spectators, including many young boys, spill out on to the pitch in an attempt to save themselves. Here we see the injured and shocked being tended by the medical services, with the police in attendance. For the record, Colin Suggett scored Sunderland's second-half equalizer having been in arrears at half-time.

Manchester United 1-2 Sunderland,
Old Trafford, 11th May 1968

Sunderland's Colin Suggett powers home a header to give Sunderland the lead at Old Trafford as Alex Stepney looks on helplessly. The Black Cats' 2-1 victory on the last day of the league season deprived the Red Devils of the First Division championship.

–LEGENDS–

Jimmy Montgomery

Holder of the record number of appearances for Sunderland AFC, Montgomery progressed from St Hilda's RC to Sunderland Boys. It is not well known that Sunderland nearly lost out on him to Burnley, with whom he spent a month's trial. But rejected by the Lancashire club, he returned home and signed for his hometown club.

Montgomery made his first-team Sunderland debut in the league cup game against Walsall on 4th October 1961, having signed professionally 10th October 1960. By the 1963/64 promotion season he had ousted Peter Wakeham in goal, making his league debut on 24th February 1962. His hobbies included playing cricket for Wearmouth.

Whilst not a tall keeper – he stood 5ft 10in – what he lacked in height he more than made up for in lightning reflexes, as the 1973 FA Cup final testified. On leaving Sunderland he won a European Cup winner's medal as a substitute for Nottingham Forest.

Montgomery gathers safely under pressure from Birmingham City's centre-forward Bob Latchford as Ritchie Pitt and Ian Porterfield look on during the opening day league encounter at Roker Park on 14th August 1971.

> *I was just a young kid who had been brought up on Sunderland. In fact I was still playing for the youth team when I suddenly found myself thrown in at the deep end. Alan Brown was the manager and Peter Wakeham was the first-team keeper. But Peter had given a V-sign to the crowd and that was it. He was dropped. It gave me my chance and I grabbed it. As a kid I had stood behind the goal at Roker Park marvelling at the agility of Johnny Bollands. He was my hero when I was a lad and how I hoped that one day I would be out there in the green jersey as Sunderland's goalkeeper.*
>
> Monty reflects on the unusual circumstances of his Sunderland debut and his love for the club

ABOVE: The wedding of Jim Montgomery and Joy Dawson at St Hilda's Church, Southwick, 26th September 1967. Celebrating with them, left to right: Colin Todd, Cecil Irwin, George Mulhall and Allan Gauden.

LEFT: Jimmy Montgomery shows off his new Chrysler 160 car in April 1973, perhaps purchased with his 1973 FA Cup-run bonus.

One of the enduring images of the 1973 FA Cup final as Sunderland manager hugs Montgomery, acknowledging his world-class heroics between the sticks.

FOOTBALL
-STATS-

Jimmy Montgomery

Name: James Montgomery

Born: Sunderland, 9th October 1943

Playing Career: 1958–1979

Clubs: Sunderland, Birmingham City, Nottingham Forest

Sunderland Appearances: 627

Born in the Fife mining town of Lochgelly, Ian Porterfield signed for Sunderland in December 1967 for a record Raith Rovers transfer fee of £45,000, having been spotted by Sunderland playing against them in a benefit game for a Fife select team. He was effectively a replacement for the recently departed Jim Baxter.

He entered Wearside folklore with perhaps the most famous and replayed goal in the history of the FA Cup. Complete underdogs going into the 1973 FA Cup final, Sunderland overcame all the odds to defeat Leeds United, then one of Europe's most feared teams. Some sterling performances following that famous day saw him on the verge of a Scotland call-up before a terrible car accident in December 1974 left him with a fractured skull and broken jaw.

Although his playing career resumed he went on to become a manager with, among others, Aberdeen, Chelsea, Zambia and Armenia. He was with the latter when he was diagnosed with colon cancer: he eventually succumbed to the disease and died a national hero in the eyes of the people of the former Soviet Satellite state. And his place as a Wearside treasure had been assured ever since that famous Cup final day in 1973.

> *We had the basis of a good team before the cup run.*
>
> Porterfield reflects on history waiting to happen

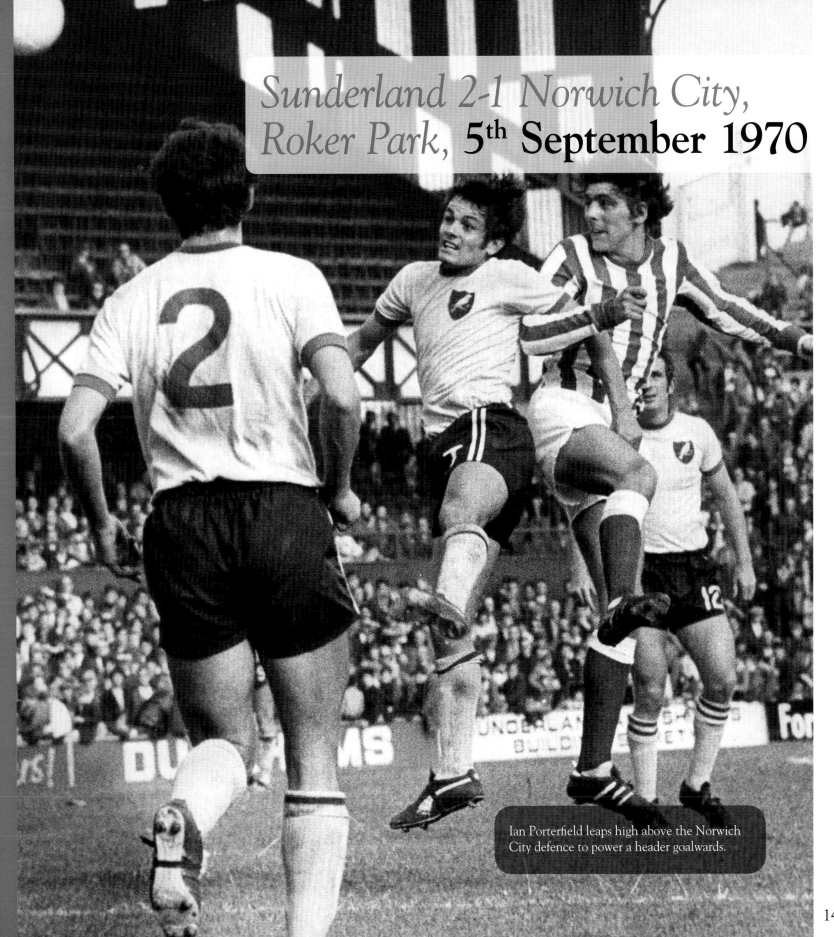

Ian Porterfield leaps high above the Norwich City defence to power a header goalwards.

Sunderland 2-1 Eintracht Frankfurt, Roker Park, 5th August 1970

Sunderland striker Billy Hughes goes head to head with the Eintracht Frankfurt goalkeeper Wolter in the pre-season friendly at Roker Park. The Black Cat scorers that day were Joe Baker and Bobby Kerr, with a lone reply from Saborowski, who had given the Germans a half-time lead. The attendance of 3,950 saw the two team's line-up as follows:

Sunderland: Montgomery, Irwin, Harvey, Todd, Heslop, McGiven, Park, Kerr, Hughes, Harris, Tueart.
Eintracht Frankfurt: Wolter, Grzye, Haedermann, Kaack, Merkhoffer, Lorenz, Gersdorff, Ulsab, Gerwein, Saborowski, Erler.

145

Sunderland AFC, *July* 1970

The Sunderland team line up at their Washington training centre in advance of the 1970/71 season. Pictured are:

Left to right, back row: Bobby Park, Bobby Kerr, Derek Forster, Colin Symm, Bruce Stuckey; centre row: Ritchie Pitt, Gordon Harris, Len Ashurst, Brian Heslop, Mike McGiven, Ian Porterfield; front row: Martin Harvey, Billy Hughes, Joe Baker, Jim Montgomery, Dennis Tueart, Colin Todd and Cecil Irwin.

147

Billy Hughes

Born in Coatbridge, Scotland, Billy was the brother of John "Yogi" Hughes, the famed Glasgow Celtic stalwart, who also played for Crystal Palace and Sunderland. His most precious Sunderland goal was probably the one scored against Arsenal in the 1973 Hillsborough semi-final, his fourth goal on the Wembley run. Here we see him in action at Roker Park against Millwall on 1st May 1971, Sunderland's last game of the 1970/71 campaign.

Legendary Supporters

John Tennick outside his house with Roker Park a mere hundred yards from his front door.

Billy Simmons outside the Supporters Association Offices, just feet away from the corner of the Clock Stand and Roker End.

For a football club with famed supporters it is hardly surprising that certain fans become deeply ingrained in the Sunderland AFC story. At Sunderland two fans became legendary because of the zeal with which they followed the Black Cats. John Tennick and Billy Simmons were both early and founding members of the Sunderland AFC Supporters Association.

Both now deceased, their passing was mourned by hundreds of their peers and to this day many Sunderland fans can vividly remember travelling on the supporters' buses, stewarded by these two Sunderland stalwarts.

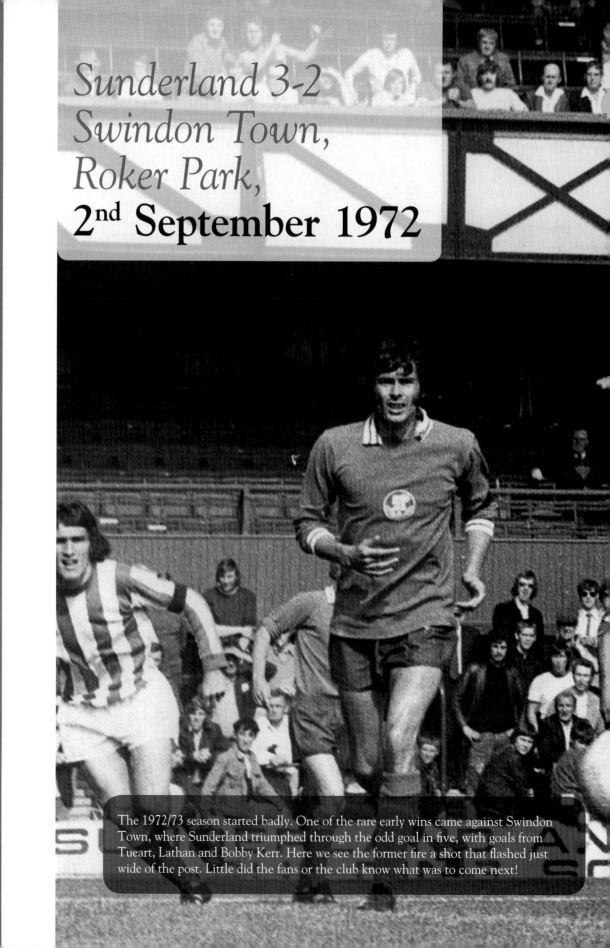

Sunderland 3-2 Swindon Town, Roker Park, 2nd September 1972

The 1972/73 season started badly. One of the rare early wins came against Swindon Town, where Sunderland triumphed through the odd goal in five, with goals from Tueart, Lathan and Bobby Kerr. Here we see the former fire a shot that flashed just wide of the post. Little did the fans or the club know what was to come next!

1973 FA Cup Run

Sunderland 2-0 Notts County, FA Cup Round 3 replay, 16th January 1973, Roker Park, Sunderland. Bobby Kerr sets up Dennis Tueart to score Sunderland's second goal. The first game at Meadow Lane had ended all square.

ABOVE: Sunderland 1-1 Reading, FA Cup Round 4, 3rd February 1973, Roker Park, Sunderland. Micky Horswill battles for the ball. With the Reading goalkeeper Steve Death in inspired form the game would go to a replay where Sunderland would triumph over Charlie Hurley's side 3-1.

Manchester City 2-2 Sunderland, FA Cup Round 5, 24th February 1973, Maine Road, Manchester. Sunderland defender Dave Watson loops a header goalwards with Rodney Marsh a spectator. Micky Horswill scores for Sunderland at Maine Road.

Sunderland 3-1 Manchester City, FA Cup Round 5 replay, 27th February 1973, Roker Park, Sunderland. A Billy Hughes piledriver at the Fulwell End makes it 2-0 to Sunderland.

Sunderland 2-0 Luton Town, FA Cup Round 6, 17th March 1973, Roker Park, Sunderland. Dave Watson is mobbed by team-mates congratulating him on scoring Sunderland's second goal. The Luton players look on in despair.

ABOVE: Arsenal 1-2 Sunderland, FA Cup semi-final, 17th April 1973, Hillsborough, Sheffield. Billy Hughes turns away having scored Sunderland's second goal. (Below) Vic Halom sets Sunderland on their way to Wembley with the first goal.

Bob Stokoe

Bob Stokoe relaxes on the beach with his daughter Karen and his dog Jed before the FA Cup final.

ABOVE: Bob Stokoe is made a
Freeman of the City in January
1974 following the club's FA Cup
final success.

LEFT: Bob Stokoe with his trademark
trilby and brown mac talks to
commentator Kenneth Wolstenholme
before the 1973 FA Cup final on the
hallowed Wembley pitch.

When Bob Stokoe was appointed as Sunderland
manager in November 1972 the side lay fourth
bottom in the Second Division with only five
wins from their first 18 league games. Knocked
out of the league cup at the first hurdle by Stoke
City, the club would then go on a journey of just
five defeats in 32 games as they won the 1973
FA Cup final against Leeds United at Wembley
Stadium to end the league season in sixth place.

Sunderland 1-0 Leeds United, Wembley Stadium, 5th May 1973

RIGHT AND BELOW: Frankie Vaughan leads the community singing before the teams are led out by their respective managers.

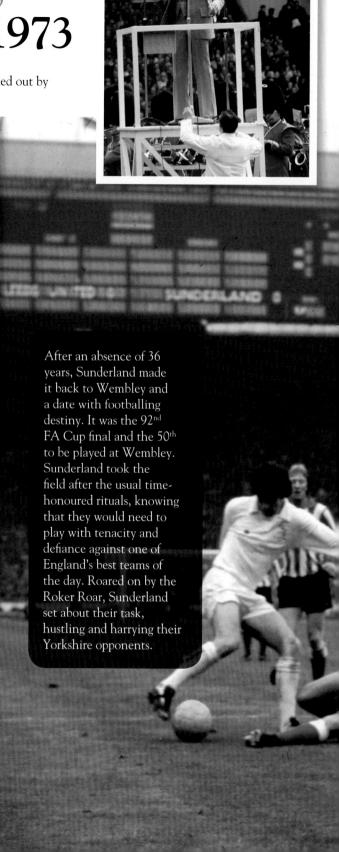

After an absence of 36 years, Sunderland made it back to Wembley and a date with footballing destiny. It was the 92nd FA Cup final and the 50th to be played at Wembley. Sunderland took the field after the usual time-honoured rituals, knowing that they would need to play with tenacity and defiance against one of England's best teams of the day. Roared on by the Roker Roar, Sunderland set about their task, hustling and harrying their Yorkshire opponents.

The outcome of the game was decided on two defining moments. On winning a corner after 31 minutes the ball was swung over, it was never dealt with by the Leeds defence, and it fell to Scotsman Ian Porterfield to smack the ball home, high into the net to send the red and white travelling hordes into delirium.

Then, midway through the second half, perhaps the most famous double save ever made at Wembley took place as Trevor Cherry saw his goal-bound header pushed away by Montgomery, only for Peter Lorimer to follow up and send an effort firmly towards the goal and an equalizer. Somehow Montgomery got to the ball and palmed it up onto the crossbar; Dick Malone, the Sunderland full-back, then smacked the ball away to safety.

Bobby Kerr holds the FA Cup aloft.

As the match drew to a close it became all too much for some. Inside the ground many Sunderland fans had to leave and pace nervously up and down the concourse, unable to watch the final minutes. At home many Sunderland fans left the comfort of their living rooms and paced in the garden.

However, finally the referee blew his whistle: Sunderland had won the FA Cup. They were the first team ever to do so at Wembley without having a current international in their team. They also became the first post-war Second Division team to take the most famous domestic club knockout trophy in the world back to their home.

Micky Horswill

Micky Horswill with three of his four sisters, Susan, Christine and Angela. A local lad, born at Annfield Plain near Stanley, County Durham, he was a tenacious player for Sunderland, winning an FA Cup winner's medal before being transferred to Manchester City in 1974, becoming good friends with the legendary Georgie Best.

–LEGENDS–

Bobby Kerr

Known as the Little General, the diminutive Bobby Kerr was the smallest winning captain in FA Cup history, and a player with great tenacity and fighting spirit. He joined Sunderland straight from school, and graduated from the youth team. Having scored the only goal of the game in his full debut against Manchester City, two broken legs were an early set back in his career.

FOOTBALL –STATS–

Bobby Kerr

Name: Robert Kerr

Born: Dumbartonshire, 16th November 1947

Playing Career: 1963–1982

Clubs: Sunderland, Blackpool, Hartlepool United

Sunderland Appearances: 432

Sunderland Goals: 69

European Cup Winners' Cup

Vic Halom tangles with the Vasas goalkeeper.

Winning the FA Cup in 1973 meant that for the first time in Sunderland's history they would compete in competitive European club football. On 19th September 1973 Sunderland travelled to the Nep Stadium in Budapest to take on Vasas of Budapest. The match resulted in a 2-0 victory, which meant that the 1-0 return triumph at Roker Park on 3rd October 1973 was expected.

Tougher opponents lay in wait, in the shape of Sporting Lisbon from Portugal. On 24th October Sunderland won the first leg 2-1 at Roker Park to take a slender lead to the José Alvalade Stadium. However, the Black Cats succumbed 0-2 in front of 50,000 spectators.

The brief European adventure was over and has yet to be repeated.

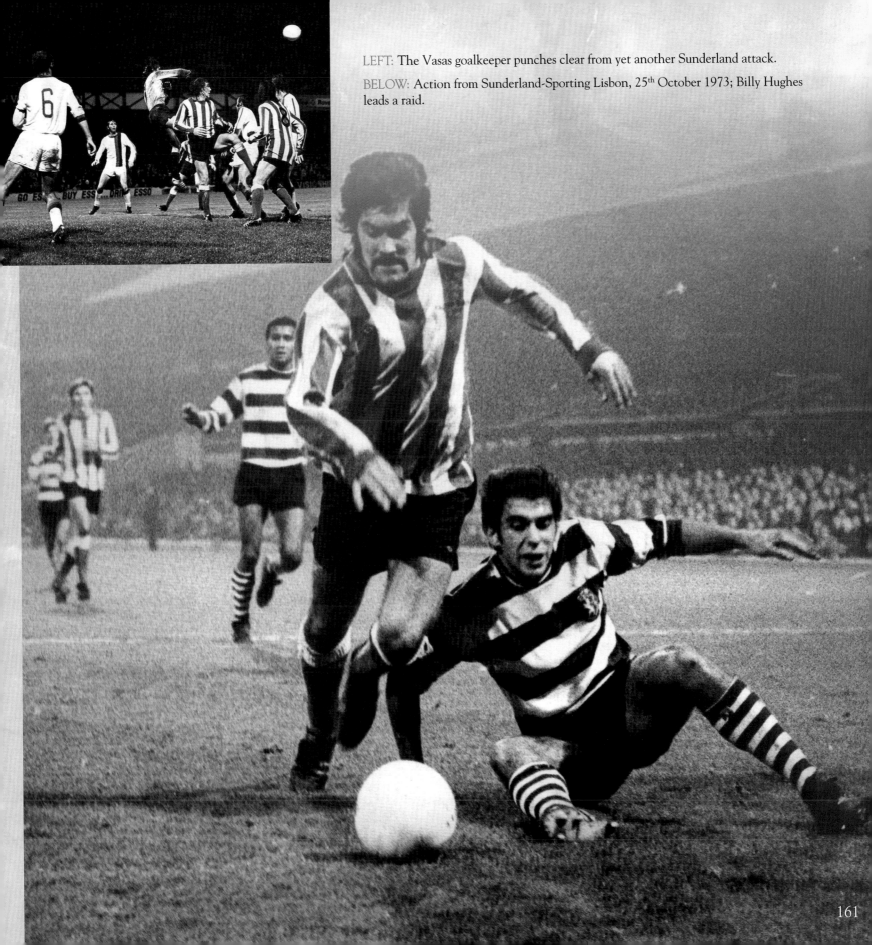

LEFT: The Vasas goalkeeper punches clear from yet another Sunderland attack.

BELOW: Action from Sunderland-Sporting Lisbon, 25th October 1973; Billy Hughes leads a raid.

161

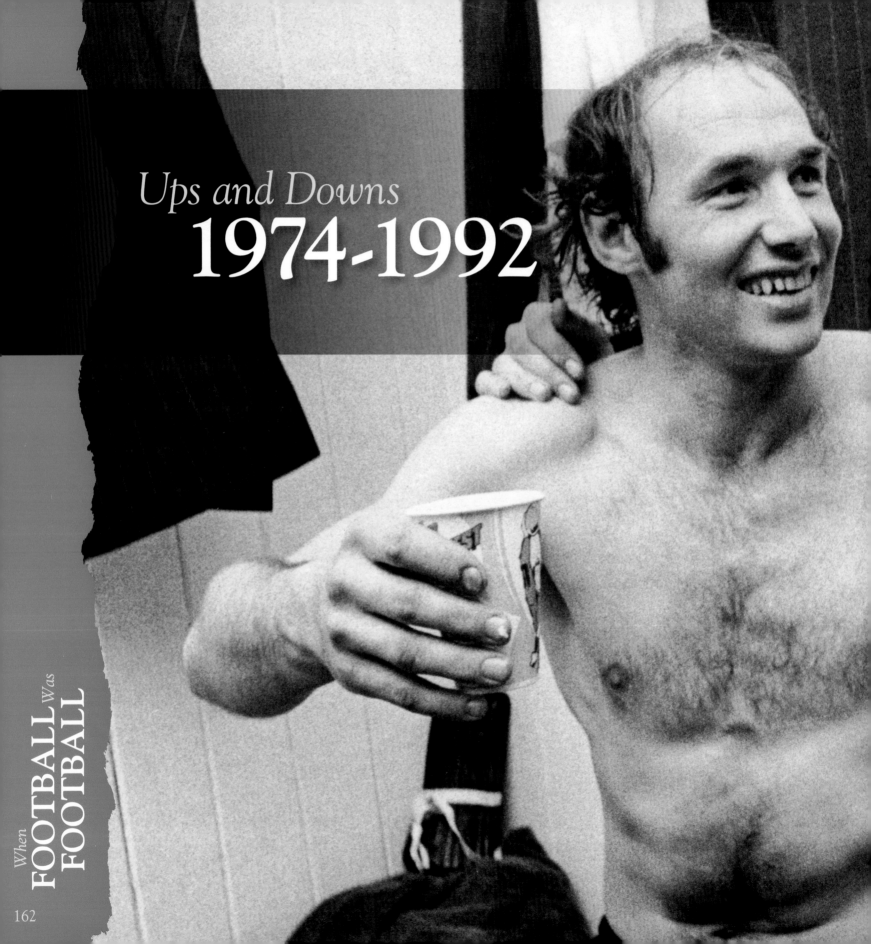

Ups and Downs
1974-1992

Pop Robson and Billy Hughes celebrate winning the 1976 Second Division title after a 2-0 victory over Portsmouth at Roker Park.

1974 Micky Horswill and Dennis Tueart play their last games for Sunderland. **1975** Sunderland miss out on promotion after a last day defeat at Villa Park. **1976** Sunderland become Second Division champions for the first time and are promoted back to the First Division. **1977** After just one season back in the top flight Sunderland are once more relegated. **1978** Gary Rowell misses his only competitive penalty against Orient. **1979** Sunderland again miss out on promotion despite winning 2-1 at Wrexham on the last day of the season. **1980** Sunderland AFC gain promotion after a last-day win at home to FA Cup winners West Ham United. **1981** Sunderland win at Anfield to maintain their top-flight status. **1983** Sunderland goalkeeper Chris Turner fractures his skull against Norwich City. **1985** Sunderland perform an unwanted double, losing the Milk Cup final to Norwich City and are relegated in the same season. **1987** Sunderland are relegated to the Third Division for the first time in their history after an away goal play-off defeat by Gillingham. **1988** Sunderland take the Third Division by storm, winning it at a canter. Promotion is sealed at Port Vale. **1990** Promoted via the play-offs, despite losing the final to Swindon Town. **1991** Sunderland relegated on the last day of the season despite the presence of 15,000 fans roaring them on at Maine Road. **1992** Sunderland reach the FA Cup final where they lose to Liverpool 0-2.

164

Sunderland players celebrate winning promotion by beating West Ham United on 12th May 1980 in front of 47,129 at Roker Park.

West Ham came to us just days after winning the cup. I remember that by 5pm the ground was full. I spoke to Stuart Pearson who had been a team-mate of mine at Hull and he told me not to worry about the game because the West Ham lads had been drinking all weekend after the cup win!

Sunderland manager Ken Knighton recounts a factor in Sunderland's 12th May 1980 victory over the Irons that sealed promotion

Mick Horswill tries to restrain Dennis Tueart as it all kicks off in the Wear–Tees derby game at Roker Park as 'Boro's Willie Maddren looks on. Although the games against the Teesside team are always hard fought affairs, in truth Sunderland's greatest rivalry will always be with Newcastle United.

Bryan "Pop" Robson dashes forward to shoot between Frank Saul and Alan Dorney of Millwall in what was the Sunderland striker's league debut for the club, as Dennis Longhorn looks on. The Black Cats won the opening day encounter with goals from Kerr, Towers, Halom and Billy Hughes. However, the fixture became infamous with the Sunderland fans in the 10,572 crowd as the unsegregated supporters fought running battles in the Main Stand.

Promotion!

The Sunderland players undertake a lap of honour following the 2-1 Roker Park victory against Bolton Wanderers on 19th April 1976 which clinches promotion for the Black Cats. Accompanying them around the pitch are some of their delighted fans.

Promotion was aided by games such as that at Boothferry Park where Sunderland ripped Hull City apart 4-1. Here a Sunderland fan runs on to the pitch to celebrate with Gary Rowell.

1976/77 – The Great Escape… Almost

Following a hard-earned promotion in the 1975/76 season the Sunderland fans were disappointed to find that by February 1977 Sunderland were rock bottom in the First Division following nine successive defeats and two draws. The tide turned on 11th February with a 1-0 home win over Bristol City. This victory set in motion one of the greatest comebacks in league history as Sunderland then scored 16 goals in just three matches, finishing off the season with only three defeats in their last 17 games. Alas, defeat at Everton and a last-day farce at Highfield Road saw Coventry City and Bristol City play out a tame draw to send Sunderland down.

19th March 1977: Colin Waldron is mobbed by his team-mates following his winner against Ipswich Town.

5th March 1977: Sunderland striker Mel Holden scores his second, a lovely header, as the Black Cats rout West Ham United 6-0.

11th April 1977: Tony Towers salutes the Roker Park crowd having scored the penalty that inflicts defeat on Manchester United.

14th May 1977: backed by over 12,000 fans who had made the long trek from Wearside to East Anglia, Sunderland found themselves 0-2 down to Norwich City at Carrow Road. Here Gary Rowell turns away having scored Sunderland's first goal with just minutes of the match remaining. The comeback was on as many red and whites who had left the ground dejected came streaming back into the stadium. Bobby Kerr would net a late equalizer.

ABOVE: 16th April 1977: Mel Holden blows a kiss to the delirious 8,000 Sunderland away support as the Black Cats snatch a precious point at White Hart Lane in their quest for survival. Shaun Elliott shares Mel's joy.

Charlton Athletic 3-2 Sunderland, The Valley, 3rd December 1977

Sunderland striker Wayne Entwhistle rises above Charlton's Peacock to score the Black Cats' second goal on his full league debut, as Gary Rowell looks on. The home side's goals were scored by Berry and Flanagan, with a Micky Henderson own-goal thrown in for good measure.

The Roker End,
17th November 1978

Sunderland reserve-team goalkeeper Ian Watson runs around the Roker Park pitch to the backdrop of the old Roker End before it was chopped down by half in the early 1980s.

West Ham United 3-3 Sunderland, Upton Park, 10th February 1979

One of the best games of the 1970s from a pure footballing perspective was witnessed when Sunderland travelled to the Boleyn Ground in February 1979 to take on West Ham United. Sunderland led an action-packed match 2-1 at half-time but eventually had to settle for a share of the points in a fabulous 3-3 draw. Despite their despairing lunges, the two Irons players pictured here can do nothing to stop local lad Wilf Rostron from slotting home the Black Cats' third goal. The Sunderland fans "enjoyed" successive away trips to West Ham United, Newcastle United and Millwall.

—LEGENDS—

Gary Rowell

Although Gary Rowell made his league debut for Sunderland in December 1975 he came to prominence in Sunderland's ultimately unsuccessful attempt to stay in the top flight during the 1976/77 campaign. In particular, the game against Leicester City at Filbert Street in January 1977 saw him line up alongside young debutants Kevin Arnott and Shaun Elliott. The combination of the three was the kick-start to an amazing three months that saw Sunderland go from relegation cannon fodder to championship form. However, Rowell made the list of Sunderland Legends in February 1979 when his first hat-trick for the club was scored against bitter rivals Newcastle United at St James' Park in a 4-1 victory. A Sunderland fan from birth, he was adored by the Roker Park faithful even after his eventual move to Norwich City.

Gary Rowell heads for goal and scores the winner again against Charlton Athletic on the opening day of the 1978/79 season at Roker Park.

ABOVE: Gary Rowell breaks through the Newcastle United defence to score at the Leazes End in his hat-trick game on 24th February 1979 and begins the 4-1 rout of the Magpies on their home patch.

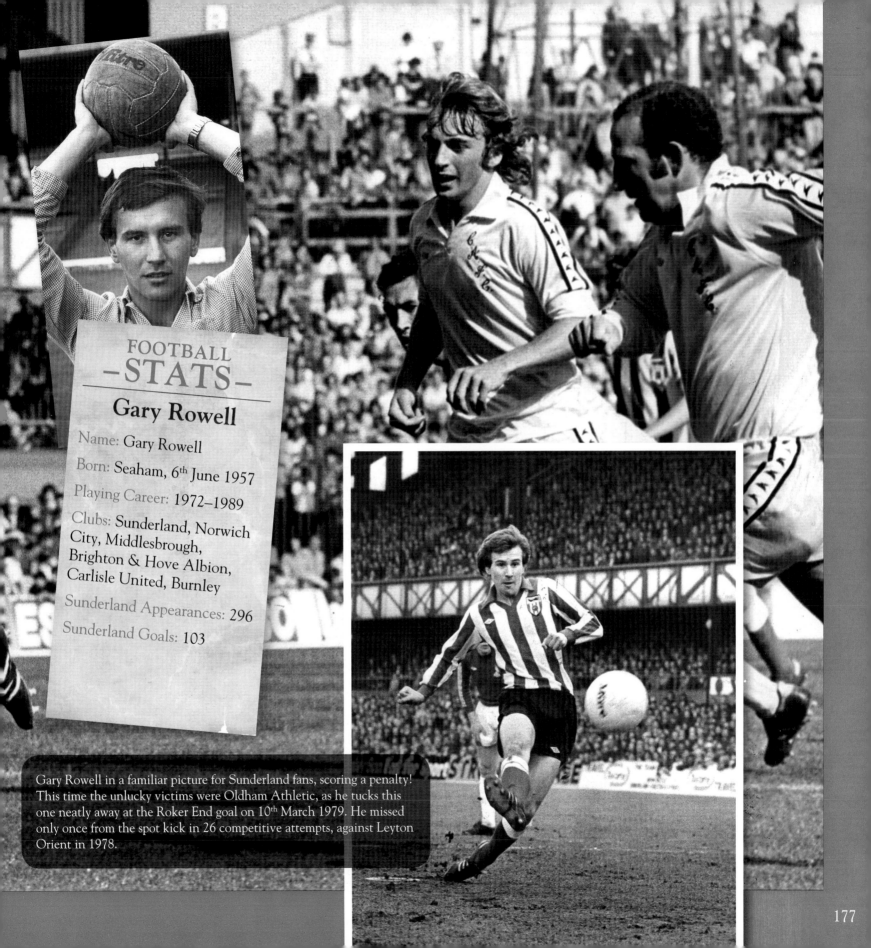

Gary Rowell in a familiar picture for Sunderland fans, scoring a penalty! This time the unlucky victims were Oldham Athletic, as he tucks this one neatly away at the Roker End goal on 10th March 1979. He missed only once from the spot kick in 26 competitive attempts, against Leyton Orient in 1978.

Sunderland midfielder Kevin Arnott bends a superb free kick at the Roker End round the Leyton Orient defensive wall to give the Black Cats a priceless point.

Sunderland 2-0 West Ham United, Roker Park, **12**th **May 1980**

The referee blows the final whistle and the fans and players celebrate promotion having defeated the Irons 2-0 in front of a packed Roker Park.

Liverpool 0-1 Sunderland, 2nd May 1981

Stan Cummins turns away at the Kop end having scored Sunderland's winner.

Sunderland went into the final day of the 1980/81 season tied with Brighton and Norwich on 33 points and equal third bottom. Whoever came out worst on their last fixture of the season would be relegated. Sunderland had the most difficult task going to Anfield to play Liverpool, who would end the season fifth. It was another tense end of season finale as far as the Black Cats and their fans were concerned, particularly the 12,000 who made the trip to Merseyside. However in the end Sunderland triumphed thanks to a goal from Stan Cummins. Safe for another season!

Sunderland players salute the 12,000 travelling fans as Black Cat supporter Gilly hugs Alan Brown, the club's No. 10 that day.

12th August 1980: Bill Pattinson, the Sunderland groundsman, tends to the Roker Park pitch on his ride-on lawnmower in advance of the red and whites' opening home game of the 1980/81 campaign against Everton four days later.

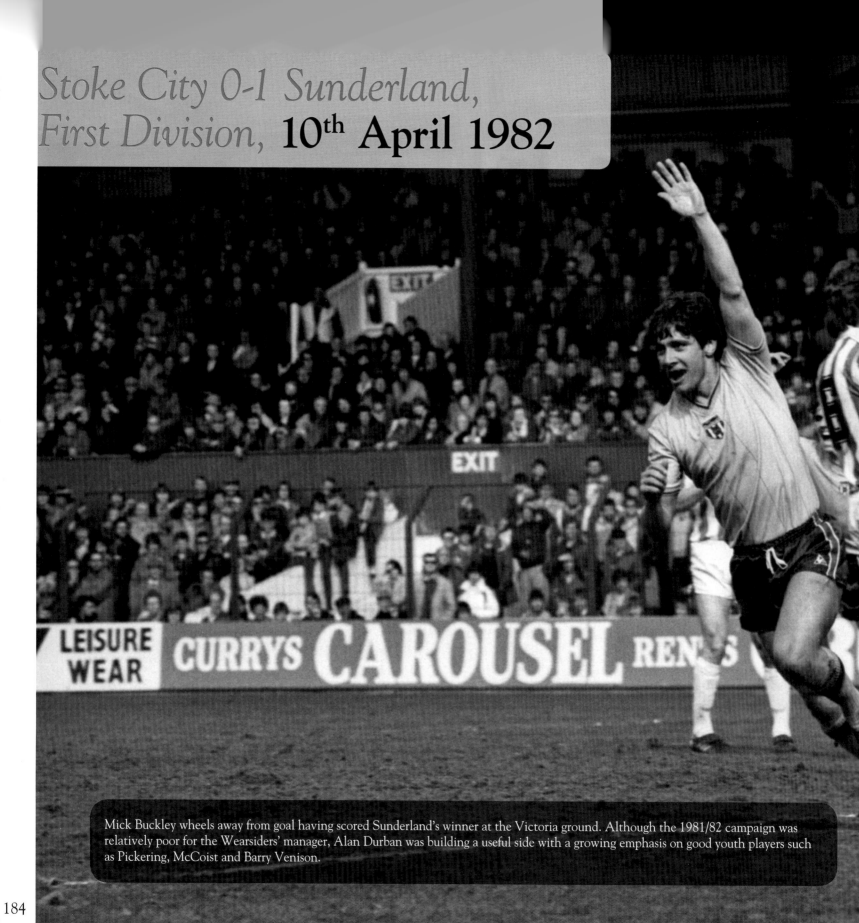

Mick Buckley wheels away from goal having scored Sunderland's winner at the Victoria ground. Although the 1981/82 campaign was relatively poor for the Wearsiders' manager, Alan Durban was building a useful side with a growing emphasis on good youth players such as Pickering, McCoist and Barry Venison.

Ally McCoist

Ally McCoist scores Sunderland's second goal against Manchester City at Maine Road on 16th October 1982.

Although Ally McCoist would eventually become a household name through his connections with Glasgow Rangers, it was with Sunderland that he initially came to prominence. Signed from St Johnstone by Alan Durban for £350,000 his goals return of nine from 46 appearances may not seem overly bountiful but his talent and potential were there for all to see. He once described the Sunderland fans as "the world's best" (football supporters).

Nissan

Sunderland manager Len Ashurst welcomes the Nissan squad to Sunderland in July 1984. Nissan were of course a major employer in the region. Sunderland played the Japanese team in a pre-season friendly on 21st July 1984 at Roker Park, winning the game 5-2, a Colin West hat-trick doing most of the damage, with Kimura and Hashiradani replying for the visitors.

–LEGENDS–

Gary Bennett

Perhaps the most cultured post-war Sunderland defender, Bennett made an immediate impact scoring on his Black Cat debut against Southampton in the opening game of the 1984/85 season at Roker Park. In a Sunderland career lasting more than 10 years he would finish with 443 appearances. Tough in the tackle and an excellent captain, he had many ups and downs on Wearside, with relegations and promotions a regular feature. Off the field he broke down cultural barriers at a time where racist abuse was a feature of terrace life. He subsequently became a leading light in the Kick Racism Out Of Football campaign and was a hugely popular figure with Sunderland fans.

Gary Bennett scores a dramatic late gasp looping header to equalize at the Fulwell End, taking the 1987 Gillingham play-off game into extra time.

THE ONE STOP OFF-LICENCE!

FOOTBALL
-STATS-

Gary Bennett

Name: Gary Ernest Bennett

Born: Manchester, 4th December 1961

Playing Career: 1979–1998

Clubs: Manchester City, Cardiff City, Sunderland, Carlisle United, Scarborough, Darlington

Sunderland Appearances: 443

Sunderland Goals: 25

One of the finest league games of the 1980s at Roker Park was the encounter with the Red Devils, a match covered by the BBC for the *Match of the Day* cameras. The Sunderland victory came courtesy of a Clive Walker hat-trick, although in this picture we see Barry Venison shooting for goal.

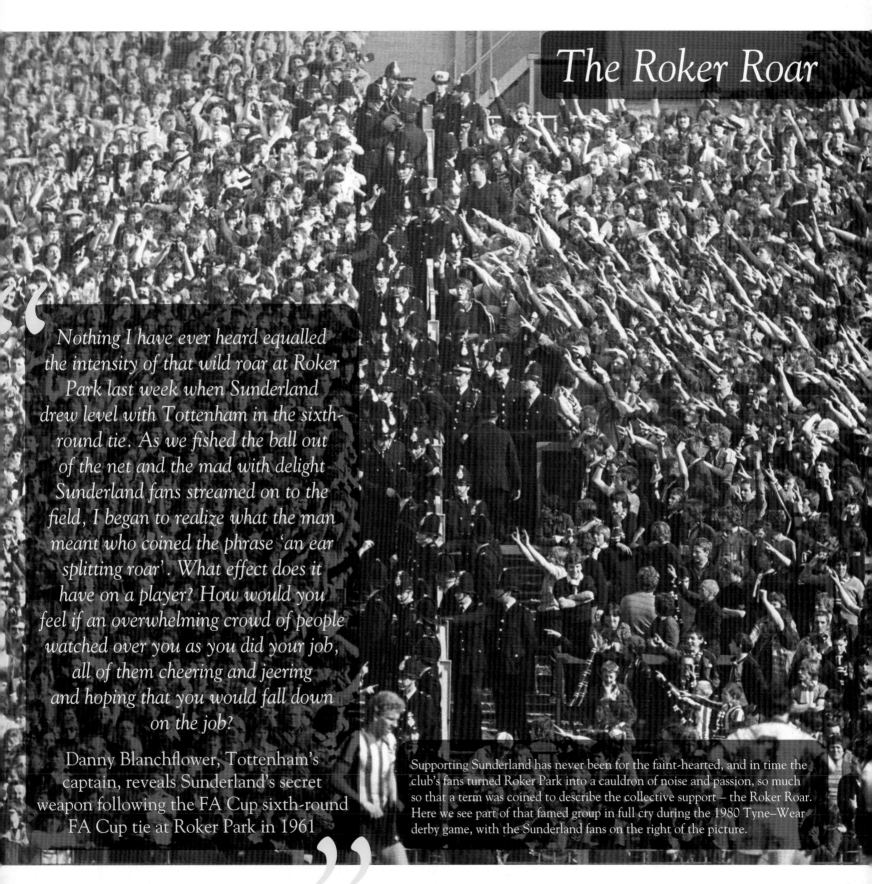

The Roker Roar

Nothing I have ever heard equalled the intensity of that wild roar at Roker Park last week when Sunderland drew level with Tottenham in the sixth-round tie. As we fished the ball out of the net and the mad with delight Sunderland fans streamed on to the field, I began to realize what the man meant who coined the phrase 'an ear splitting roar'. What effect does it have on a player? How would you feel if an overwhelming crowd of people watched over you as you did your job, all of them cheering and jeering and hoping that you would fall down on the job?

Danny Blanchflower, Tottenham's captain, reveals Sunderland's secret weapon following the FA Cup sixth-round FA Cup tie at Roker Park in 1961

Supporting Sunderland has never been for the faint-hearted, and in time the club's fans turned Roker Park into a cauldron of noise and passion, so much so that a term was coined to describe the collective support – the Roker Roar. Here we see part of that famed group in full cry during the 1980 Tyne–Wear derby game, with the Sunderland fans on the right of the picture.

Norwich City 1-0 Sunderland, Milk Cup final, **24th March 1985**

Sunderland players Steve Berry, Nick Pickering, Chris Turner and David Corner ready to board the coach that would eventually take them to Wembley for the 1985 Milk Cup final against Norwich City at Wembley Stadium. In what turned out to be a debacle for the Black Cats, Sunderland's Gordon Chisholm would feel the ball ricochet off his back and nestle into his own net to hand the East Anglian side the trophy. To make matters worse, Clive Walker missed a penalty for Sunderland. Ironically (see inset) Sunderland had defeated Norwich City in a league match at Carrow Road just one week before the final.

With Sunderland in deep relegation trouble and in danger of going into the Third Division, the club turned to the only man capable of getting them out of trouble, "The Messiah", Bob Stokoe. Stokoe made an emotional return to the Roker Park hot seat at Valley Parade, the home of Bradford City, still wearing his trademark trilby. Here a devoted Sunderland fan shakes hands with the man himself.

Sunderland 4-3 Gillingham,
Roker Park, **14th May 1987**

194

Tony Cascarino scores the goal at the Roker End that effectively seals Sunderland's relegation into the third tier of English football.

Sunderland AFC had teetered on the brink of football ignominy for most of the 1986/87 season, but when relegation to the Third Division became a reality the enormity of the club's troubles became apparent.

Having missed a penalty and given away a lead against Barnsley at Roker Park in Sunderland's final Second Division game of the season, the Black Cats had to negotiate a tricky home and away play-off trial against Gillingham. A narrow 2-3 reverse at Priestfield meant that Sunderland only had to win 1-0 to save themselves, but on 14th May 1987 they couldn't pull it off. They did win, but the 4-3 margin meant that the Kent side relegated Sunderland, on away goals – trust Sunderland!

The demise of this famous football club was complete.

Sunderland's cause wasn't helped by a penalty miss by Mark Proctor.

Third Division Promotion

Sunderland's reaction to their demotion was simple: they set about demolishing the teams that were put in front of them. Promotion was won at the first time of asking and confirmed courtesy of an Eric Gates goal at Port Vale on 30th April 1988. For the Sunderland fans who saw it all, particularly those who travelled away from home, it was on reflection a season to remember. The trophy was collected at the following home game against Northampton Town on 2nd May 1988.

Sunderland players line up in the Fulwell End on 12th April 1988 as they parade the suits they will wear for the Mercantile Credit Football Festival. The tournament, which took place at Wembley, was by invitation only to celebrate the centenary of the Football League. Sunderland, the Third Division representatives, drew 0-0 with Wigan Athletic and lost on penalties. The competition was won outright by Nottingham Forest.

–LEGENDS–

Marco Gabbiadini

One of the bright spots of the Third Division campaign was the signing of Marco Gabbiadini from York City by his mentor Denis Smith for a transfer fee of £80,000. Gabbiadini's signing was seen as risky, since in order to raise funds to sign him Smith had to sell one of Sunderland's most popular players, midfielder Mark Proctor, to Sheffield Wednesday. Gabbiadini made his Sunderland debut in the 2-0 defeat to Chester City. In the following match he scored his first two goals against Fulham. He would quickly establish himself as a key player and a crowd favourite for Sunderland by scoring on a regular basis.

If Gabbiadini had an Achilles heel it was his disciplinary record; yet the fans would forgive him anything, particularly after he scored Sunderland's second at St James' Park to send arc-rivals Newcastle United packing in the 1990 Second Division league play-off semi-final.

Shortly after the start of the 1991/92 season, Gabbiadini was sold to Crystal Palace for a club record transfer fee of £1.8million. He was seen by the Eagles as a replacement for Ian Wright.

Marco Gabbiadini with his bride Deborah Warren on the occasion of their wedding in June 1991. The best man, Marco's younger brother Ricardo, raises his hat in celebration.

Marco in typical pose as he raises his arms in triumph to celebrate yet another goal for Sunderland.

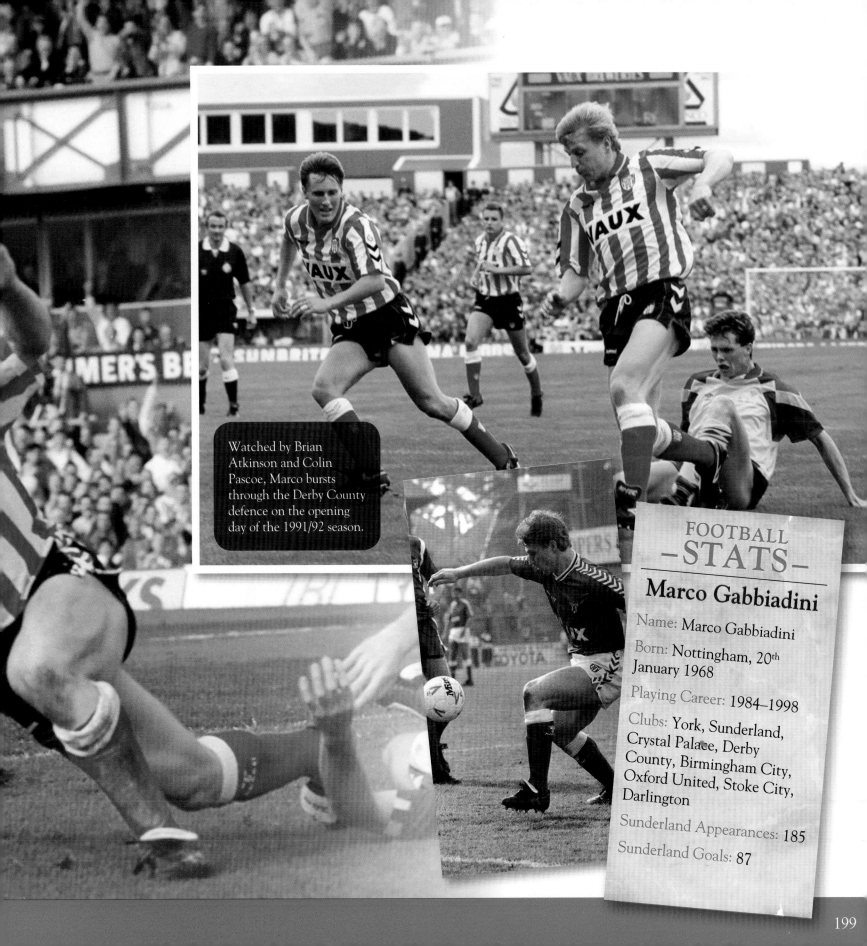

Watched by Brian Atkinson and Colin Pascoe, Marco bursts through the Derby County defence on the opening day of the 1991/92 season.

FOOTBALL —STATS—

Marco Gabbiadini

Name: Marco Gabbiadini

Born: Nottingham, 20th January 1968

Playing Career: 1984–1998

Clubs: York, Sunderland, Crystal Palace, Derby County, Birmingham City, Oxford United, Stoke City, Darlington

Sunderland Appearances: 185

Sunderland Goals: 87

Pre-season Training

The Sunderland squad are put through their pre-season paces at Maiden Castle, Durham, 20th July 1988, in advance of the new league campaign.

The Charlie Hurley Centre

In 1959 Sunderland AFC bought land at Cleadon near Whitburn in south Tyneside as a training ground for the club's players. It was upgraded and modernized in 1990 and became known as the Charlie Hurley Centre. Here we see the man himself opening the facility in 1990.

Newcastle United 0-2 Sunderland, semi-final play-off, St James' Park, 16th May 1990

Eric Gates congratulates Marco Gabbiadini after scoring Sunderland's second goal in the play-off victory against Newcastle United at St James' Park. In the background, and much to the delight of the Sunderland supporters, the Magpie fans are on the verge of invading the pitch.

Swindon Town 1-0 Sunderland, Wembley Stadium, play-off final, **27th May 1990**

Steve White celebrates after his shot is deflected into the Sunderland net. John Kay and Tony Norman are crestfallen.

Following the now legendary win over bitter rivals Newcastle United at St James' Park, Sunderland won through to a Wembley play-off final against Swindon Town for the right to play in the First Division. Sunderland played poorly, lost the game 0-1, but were reprieved when Swindon were denied promotion because of financial irregularities.

Those few days in May 1990 sum up the rollercoaster ride that the football club and the fans endured.

-LEGENDS-

Kevin Ball

Eventual club captain of Sunderland AFC, Kevin Ball arrived on Wearside from Portsmouth, when then manager Denis Smith paid £350,000 for him in the summer of 1990 to replace John McPhail. An excellent reader of the game, quick off the mark and a determined tackler, there would be few opponents who relished a 50/50 with Ball. He was Sunderland's player of the year in his first season at the club. He made his Pompey debut against Shrewsbury in 1984, amassing 128 appearances for the south coast club as a defender, although he subsequently was turned into a midfield ball winner at Sunderland. An extremely popular player on Wearside, he was a member of the club's 1992 FA Cup final side and made many appearances for the Black Cats.

FOOTBALL
–STATS–

Kevin Ball

Name: Kevin Anthony Ball

Born: Hastings, 12th November 1964

Playing Career: 1982–2002

Clubs: Portsmouth, Sunderland, Fulham, Burnley

Sunderland Appearances: 388

Sunderland Goals: 27

Liverpool 2-0 Sunderland, 1992 FA Cup final, Wembley Stadium, 9th May 1992

The 1992 FA Cup final was the fourth time Liverpool and Sunderland had met in the competition, with the Merseysiders just shading it 2-1. In 1921/22 the teams had played out a 1-1 draw, with Liverpool winning the replay 5-0. In 1960/61 Sunderland won a fourth-round tie at Anfield 2-0, and in 1981/82 Liverpool had won 3-0 at Roker Park. For Liverpool's 10th final, Sunderland's fourth, the Scousers were the overwhelming favourites.

In the 111th FA Cup final, John Byrne was trying to join a small band of players who had scored in every round, and in the first half he had a glorious chance; but luck would desert him this day. Bracewell also had a good shot, but deflected just wide.

In the second half, even the double-banking of MacManaman by Rogan and Armstrong couldn't prevent Liverpool running riot, and it came as no surprise when a spectacular effort by Michael Thomas put the Merseysiders one up and firmly in the driving seat. Ian Rush added a second with 24 minutes remaining.

There was no disgrace for Sunderland, who had put up a great show, but in the end the club were quite simply beaten by the better team on the day. It was an ideal present for manager Graeme Souness, who had just come out of hospital after heart bypass surgery.

Sunderland were greeted home by tens of thousands of people who acknowledged once more that the team had nearly triumphed against all the odds.

The Sunderland fans roar on their team.

LEFT: Sunderland fans soak up the Wembley atmosphere outside the stadium.

BELOW: Malcolm Crosby leads the Sunderland players on to the pitch alongside their Liverpool counterparts.

ABOVE: Sunderland dangerman John Byrne is watched closely by two Liverpool defenders.

LEFT: Gordon Armstrong rises above Mark Wright as Gary Bennett looks on.

BELOW LEFT: It's all over. Sunderland lose but are far from disgraced as they take a bow on a lap of honour.

BELOW: Welcome home. The Sunderland team are greeted like winners following their FA Cup-run heroics.

For William Days, "Uncle Billy", 1939–2008, gone but never forgotten

The author would like to thank:

Richard Havers for his patience and for always being on the end of the phone. David Scripps and the team at Mirrorpix Watford archive. Ann Dixon at the northeast archive.

Also thanks to Paul Joannou for his sound advice.